Lenin's Revolution:
Russia, 1917–1921

We work with leading authors to develop the
strongest educational materials in history,
bringing cutting-edge thinking and best learning
practice to a global market.

Under a range of well-known imprints, including
Longman, we craft high-quality print and electronic
publications which help readers to understand and
apply their content, whether studying or at work.

To find out more about the complete range of our
publishing please visit us on the World Wide Web at:
www.pearsoneduc.com

SEMINAR STUDIES   IN HISTORY

Lenin's Revolution:
Russia, 1917–1921

DAVID R. MARPLES

An imprint of **Pearson** Education

Harlow, England · London · New York · Reading, Massachusetts · San Francisco · Toronto · Don Mills, Ontario · Sydney
Tokyo · Singapore · Hong Kong · Seoul · Taipei · Cape Town · Madrid · Mexico City · Amsterdam · Munich · Paris · Milan

Pearson Education Limited
Edinburgh Gate
Harlow
Essex CM20 2JE
England
and Associated Companies throughout the world.

Visit us on the World Wide Web at:
www.pearsoneduc.com

First published 2000

© Pearson Education Limited 2000

ISBN 0-582-31917-X PPR

British Library Cataloguing-in-Publication Data
A catalogue record for this book is
available from the British Library

Library of Congress Cataloging-in-Publication Data
Marples, David R.
    Lenin's revolution: Russia, 1917–1921 / David R. Marples.
      p. cm. -- (Seminar studies in history)
    Includes bibliographical references and index.
    ISBN 0-582-31917-X (PPR)
      1. Soviet Union--History--Revolution, 1917–1921. I. Title. II. Series.

DK265.M3153 2000
947.084'1--dc21   00-040535

Set by 7 in 10/12 Sabon Roman
Printed in Malaysia, KVP

For Yuri and Zena Risovanny

CONTENTS

INTRODUCTION TO THE SERIES

Such is the pace of historical enquiry in the modern world that there is an ever-widening gap between the specialist article or monograph, incorporating the results of current research, and general surveys, which inevitably become out of date. Seminar Studies in History are designed to bridge this gap. The series was founded by Patrick Richardson in 1966 and his aim was to cover major themes in British, European and world history. Between 1980 and 1996 Roger Lockyer continued his work, before handing the editorship over to Clive Emsley and Gordon Martel. Clive Emsley is Professor of History at the Open University, while Gordon Martel is Professor of International History at the University of Northern British Columbia, Canada, and Senior Research Fellow at De Montfort University.

All the books are written by experts in their field who are not only familiar with the latest research but have often contributed to it. They are frequently revised, in order to take account of new information and interpretations. They provide a selection of documents to illustrate major themes and provoke discussion, and also a guide to further reading. The aim of Seminar Studies is to clarify complex issues without over-simplifying them, and to stimulate readers into deepening their knowledge and understanding of major themes and topics.

NOTE ON REFERENCING SYSTEM

Readers should note that numbers in square brackets [5] refer them to the corresponding entry in the Bibliography at the end of the book (specific page numbers are given in italics). A number in square brackets preceded by *Doc.* [*Doc. 5*] refers readers to the corresponding item in the Documents section which follows the main text.

NOTE ON DATING

This book adheres throughout to the Gregorian or New Style calendar introduced by Pope Gregory XIII in 1582. By the mid-eighteenth century, most European countries had adopted this calendar. Russia, however, used the Julian calendar until 1918. That calendar misread the length of the solar year, which led the calendar dates of the seasons to lose one day each century. By the time of the Russian Revolution, the Julian calendar used by Russia was thirteen days behind that of the West. Thus the October Revolution (25 October 1917) actually took place on 7 November 1917 according to the Gregorian calendar.

PREFACE

My aim in writing this book was to provide a synthesis of the Russian Revolution to assist university, college and high school students. I have tried to take into account the most recent and incisive works, though like any historian, I have been hampered somewhat by the lack of consensus on many issues. My reliance has been primarily on western secondary works rather than Russian or Soviet ones. The end of the Soviet Union saw the opening of some of the Russian archives and, for a brief spell, the publication of a variety of new works on Lenin and the revolutions of 1917. Russian works, however, have been few, and they are not always reliable as they are written either with a distinctly political hue (D. Volkogonov, for example) or with an eye for the dramatic (as in the case of the work of E. Radzinsky).

I have taught the Russian Revolution for the past seven years at the University of Alberta and in writing this book have kept in mind some of the questions raised by my students and the issues they found most difficult to comprehend. In the vastness of its scope, the Russian Revolution is similar to the Second World War. The student needs something on which to focus, to provide an explanation of the bewildering events. I decided to focus primarily on Lenin as the main architect of the revolution of November and a man who imposed his singular stamp on the Soviet state. As with all personalities, Lenin's was not static and this work has argued that the principal change occurred between the period of opposition and that of taking power. Most of the events of 1918–21 can be explained largely by the intransigence and ruthlessness of the Bolshevik leadership, and Lenin in particular.

I would like to express my gratitude to Gordon Martel, chairman of the History Programme at the University of Northern British Columbia, who is the Editor of this series, and also to Emma Mitchell, my Senior Acquisitions Editor at Longman. Both have shown patience and have been ready with ideas and guidance when required. I am thankful also to my graduate student Kim Palmer for her help in the final weeks of preparation, and to two other graduate students in the Department of History and Classics, University of Alberta, who worked very capably as my research assistants in the early stages of the project: Kryszstof Lada and Srja Pavlovic.

David R. Marples
Edmonton, Canada
March 2000

ACKNOWLEDGEMENTS

Plates 1–8 are reproduced by permission of David King Collection.

We are grateful to the University of Michigan Press for permission to reproduce an extract from *Political Memoirs, 1905–1917* by Milyukov © The University of Michigan Press 1967.

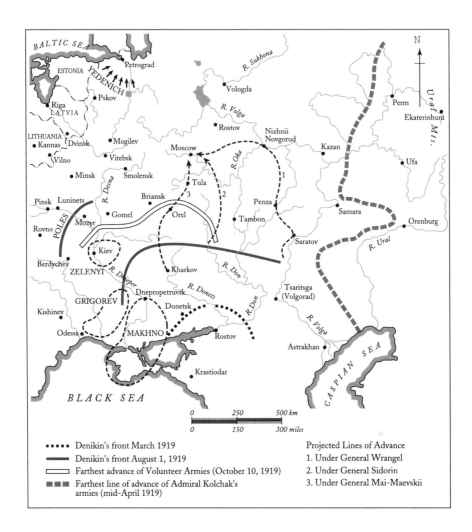

Legend:

- ▪▪▪▪▪ Denikin's front March 1919
- ▬▬▬ Denikin's front August 1, 1919
- ▭ Farthest advance of Volunteer Armies (October 10, 1919)
- ▰▰▰ Farthest line of advance of Admiral Kolchak's armies (mid-April 1919)

Projected Lines of Advance
1. Under General Wrangel
2. Under General Sidorin
3. Under General Mai-Maevskii

Map 1   The Russian Civil War, 1919

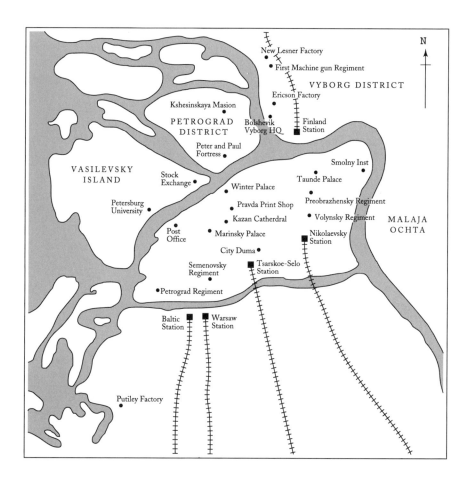

Map 2   Revolutionary Petrograd

PART ONE   BACKGROUND

CHAPTER ONE

PRELUDE TO REVOLUTION

EARLY REVOLUTIONARY MOVEMENTS

According to Soviet historiography, a Russian revolutionary tradition began in 1825 with the Decembrist revolt and continued until the Great October Socialist Revolution of 1917, when Lenin and the Bolshevik Party were swept to power on the arms of the masses. In reality there was no discernible continual movement. The fuel for the revolutionary movements of the 1860s and 1870s was essentially peasant discontent with the existing order, and particularly the aftermath of the abolition of serfdom in 1861. In the early years of the reign of Aleksandr II, Herzen wielded exceptional influence through his journal *Kolokol* (The Bell), which was published in London, where the philosopher was living. Those most affected were student intellectuals, many of whom had been educated abroad and returned to Russia full of ideas and zeal with which to transform their 'backward' native society. Serfdom was Herzen's main target. Even after the Act of Emancipation, no upheaval was feasible in Russia without the participation of the rural element. In addition, under the influence of the military officer P.I. Lavrov, the revolutionaries were imbued with the idea that they owed a debt to society and to the peasants in particular. It was Lavrov who coined the slogan 'To the people', which inspired the movement of the educated urban elite into the countryside to educate the peasants and fill them with the spirit of revolution. These activists were termed Narodniki (Populists).

In 1873–74 this movement began in earnest, but by all accounts it was an abject failure. The Russian peasants, superstitious and wary of visitors from outside their villages, often detained the idealists and handed them over to the local police. Once the tsarist authorities learned of the 'intrusions', arrests were widespread and those that managed to escape were obliged to consider alternatives for the continuation of the revolutionary struggle. In 1878 an organization was formed called Land and Liberty (Zemlya i Volya), which was probably the closest that Russia had had to a workable revolutionary society to date and which carried out several violent actions in the cities against officials, particularly in St Petersburg. However, there was little consensus among the members of Land and Liberty as to how best to bring about a social revolution in Russia.

A key question was whether Russia could overthrow the autocratic system while remaining a peasant country. Many revolutionaries believed that this was possible. Russia, it was argued, could base its revolution on the village community, the utopian organization that was already in place and responsible for the administration of the villages in post-serfdom Russia. Others maintained that under the harsh authoritarian conditions of Russia, their best hope was to resort to terrorism and specifically the ass-assination of the tsar in order to bring about societal change. By 1879, therefore, the Land and Liberty movement had experienced a rift between the would-be terrorists and those who maintained their faith in the village as the catalyst for revolutionary change. The former group became known as the People's Will (Narodnaya Volya) and the latter was known as Black Repartition (Chernyi Peredel'). Initially the People's Will achieved most attention and established a terrorist tradition that was to continue in Russia into the twentieth century. They sought to remove the existing government with a revolution that would take place in both countryside and town. There was nothing deterministic in their view. Simply put, they felt that the people could be united against the harsh ruling autocracy. Naively, they believed that the main key to change was the removal of the person, rather than the institution, of the tsar.

There was an element of farce about the assassination of Aleksandr II on 1 March 1881, but it was an important event. It provided the revolutionaries with their first real success. But it also demonstrated to those revolutionaries who came after them the sheer futility of pursuing such a policy in the future. Aleksandr was killed by a primitive bomb, thrown at the second attempt by a revolutionary called Grinevitsky, while showing a remarkable disregard for his own safety. The People's Will had planned the assassination for weeks and meticulously selected a small group to carry out the act, but after the death of Aleksandr, the young revolutionaries were rounded up and their leaders executed. Never again did the People's Will attain such prominence as in March 1881. That time proved to be both their heyday and death knell. In 1887, when an effort was made to revive the terrorist tradition and remove Aleksandr III on the sixth anniversary of the death of his father, the plot was rapidly uncovered and the ringleaders (including the elder brother of V.I. Lenin, Aleksandr Ulyanov) were hanged. The reign of Aleksandr III is often described as one of the most reactionary periods in Russian history.

Despite the failure of Populism and the grievances engendered by the Act of Emancipation, the noble landowners suffered more setbacks than the peasants in the latter years of the century. Many went bankrupt and left the land, which was then taken over by the peasants themselves or else by those who came from the towns. By the time of the First World War, peasants and former peasants possessed about 90 per cent of the land in the Russian Empire. The complaints, however, continued, and the peasants were anxious to acquire the remainder of the land. They played an increasing role in overall state production of grain but suffered from overpopulation in the European part of the empire. As for the nobles, clearly some benefited by moving to the cities, running businesses and forming new careers. Many others felt alienated from society, particularly from a new class of entrepreneurs that had begun to play an increasing role in the government.

In the last two decades of the century particularly harsh measures were directed against the Jewish population, especially those living in the Pale of Settlement in the western part of the empire. Living conditions there were bleak. Most Jews, who made up a majority or plurality of the population in the major cities (Wilno, Grodno, Minsk, for example), were confined to ghettos and were not permitted to travel outside them. When riots and demonstrations broke out against the Jews in the 1880s, the government made no effort to stop them. Both Aleksandr III and his son Nikolay II were anti-Semites and the reign of the latter was a particularly cruel one for the Jewish population. It has been estimated that there were about 5 million Jews living in the Russian Empire by the end of the nineteenth century. They can be described as a persecuted and distinct minority, and many of the younger generation found their way into the revolutionary movement, one of the few ways to circumvent anti-Jewish pograms and official restrictions on career opportunities [99].

The existence of large minorities in a contiguous empire was particularly important for the birth of the revolutionary movement in Russia. A revolutionary movement could count on a high degree of cooperation from the non-Russians of the empire. Populism, however, had failed manifestly by the reign of Aleksandr III. Marxism, the leading revolutionary current in Europe, had barely begun to penetrate the vast Russian lands. It was primarily an urban phenomenon. However, as Russia experienced a dramatic surge in industrial development and with the manifest decline of Populism, Marxism began to gain in appeal. One reason for the growth of an extremist doctrine was the relative weakness of Russian liberalism because of the small and undeveloped middle class in Russia. Nevertheless, such a liberal tradition did exist, initially in the Russian emigration in Germany.

The major liberal group in Russia was the Constitutional Democrats, better known by the Russian abbreviation, Kadets. The Kadets were formed in the autumn of 1905 during the revolution of that year, but their origins lay in a group of Russian exiles based in Stuttgart. This group, led by the former Marxist Petr Struve, founded a journal called *Liberation* in an effort to attract reformers who were alienated from Marxism and the class struggle. Subsequently a Union of Liberation was formed which ultimately united with the Zemstvo Constitutionalists to create the Kadet Party. This party proved to be quite durable but it has not always received a favourable press, partly because with the leftward evolution of the political climate in Russia, the Kadets came to represent the hardened property-owning classes trying to stem the tide of revolution. In 1905, however, their policies were moderate and progressive, advocating a constitutional monarchy, the promotion of civil liberties, the abolition of any kind of discrimination based on race, the better treatment of the urban poor, and even the transferral of private land to the peasants, albeit with appropriate compensation to the landowners. Progressive though these tenets may have been in 1905, they seemed seriously outdated in 1917. Nonetheless, the Kadets weathered the tide of change considerably better than most other parties.

The heirs of the Russian Populist tradition formed the Social Revolutionary Party in 1900. The party, known as the SRs, was the largest party in Russia at the time of the 1917 revolutions but was lacking in discipline and organization, and had an indecisive leadership. Often there was little connection between the leadership of the party in St Petersburg and the rank and file in the countryside. The SRs maintained the terrorist traditions of the People's Will [22] and also had some links with anarchists, particularly among sailors of the Baltic Fleet. The goal of the SRs was the transformation of Russia into a socialist society and one important instrument was to be a Constituent Assembly that would, under their direction, resolve the land question in their favour. The most prominent SR was Viktor Chernov, a trained lawyer from Moscow State University.

LENIN: BACKGROUND AND VIEWS

V.I. Ulyanov (Lenin) was born into a family of petty nobility in Simbirsk on 22 April 1870. He has been one of the most frequently discussed personalities in contemporary literature, and even since the dissolution of the Soviet Union in December 1991, the spate of biographies has continued [36; 39]. The harshest analyses depict him as a vindictive and ruthless tyrant who played a less than glorious role in the October Revolution and was even a coward. The most laudatory remain those written in the Soviet era when Lenin acquired the mantle of a deity, one whose views could not be questioned and whose way of life was a model for all Soviet citizens. For at least 20 years there has been a debate over whether Lenin's revolution paved the way for Stalin's cruel and bureaucratic regime which persecuted millions of Soviet citizens. Even with the uncovering of new archival information it is fair to say that this question has not been resolved. One problem is that it is difficult to discern how Lenin would have governed a state in peacetime, in good health, and with a stable economy. These three key factors never occurred during the period 1917–24.

Lenin's background can be described as bourgeois. The family was relatively affluent, though all the children became revolutionaries. His father, a school inspector in the province of Simbirsk, was a member of the Russian nobility. Lenin's ancestry was mixed, containing Russian, Kalmyk, Jewish, Swedish and German elements. He appears to have looked up to his older brother Aleksandr, but to have lacked Aleksandr's pleasant personality and good nature. Soviet versions of Lenin's life maintain that he became a revolutionary upon the execution of Aleksandr in 1887 [57], a myth perpetuated after Lenin's death by his wife, Nadezhda Krupskaya. Until 1887, however, Lenin appears to have been an exceptional, even a model student. The first record of his partaking in revolutionary activities dates from the autumn of that year when he was expelled from the Faculty of Law at Kazan University. Such expulsions were not infrequent among Lenin's contemporaries.

By 1889 Lenin was acquainted with the writings of Marx, including *Das Kapital*, and he made contact with some of the Russian-based Marxists. In this same year the family moved to Samara, where Lenin both completed his law degree, achieving first class honours, and began to practice as a lawyer. This was a period of his life that was not given much attention in Soviet works. Lenin, already balding, was a small stocky man with reddish hair and Mongolian features. He had an incisive and analytical mind and a domineering nature. It was less his originality than the forceful way in which he projected his ideas that made him a powerful figure. In addition his practicality and flexibility came to be key factors in his later career. He was a much better judge of a political situation than his peers. Some writers have declared that through working in the legal system he came to perceive its subjective nature and the way it favoured the privileged classes. Lenin, however, would have seen that from the outset and there seems to have been something intensely personal in his political posturing.

When did Lenin become a Marxist? The answer seems to be at some point in 1889, at the age of 19. In 1893 he moved to the capital, St Petersburg, where he became better acquainted with the political climate and Marxist circles. Two years later he travelled to western Europe where he met the revered leader of the Russian Marxists, Grigorii Plekhanov, a man who was to retain a significant influence over Lenin even in the days when they had parted ways politically. When he returned to St Petersburg, Lenin seems to have stepped up his political activity as an emissary for this older group of exiled Marxists. Together with his friend Yuly Tsederbaum (Martov), he began to incite the workers to take action. The tsarist authorities arrested and imprisoned both Lenin and Martov, before sending them into exile in Siberia during the period 1897–1900. During this exile, Lenin married his political comrade and faithful ally Nadezhda Krupskaya, a woman of Jewish background. He was allowed comforts that would become unimaginable in the Soviet Union during Stalin's leadership, and this period of exile appears to have been a formative and constructive period of his life, when he was able to take the time to examine the economic development of Russia and the role therein of his party, the Russian Social Democratic Workers' Party (RSDWP). Living in the village of Shushenskoye, Yeniseysk province, Lenin and Krupskaya were able to write and communicate freely, and even received a stipend from the government.

During his Siberian exile Lenin wrote and published his most original book, entitled *The Development of Capitalism in Russia*. This anticipated the increasing stratification of the Russian peasantry, and the eventual alliance of the poorer stratum with the working class (proletariat). The system of the village community would be destroyed by capitalist development and thus could not serve – as the Populists had maintained – as the basis for a social revolution in Russia. Lenin despised the Populists (paradoxically a group much favoured by Marx himself), believing that their goals for the village would result in small-scale peasant capitalism through the village communities. Lenin's other main target during these last years of the nineteenth century was the group known as the Economists, who, in his view, were perverting the laws of Marxism with an argument that the plight of workers could be alleviated by legal means, through trade union and other agitation to secure appropriate social benefits from the state. Lenin believed that such views were highly dangerous because they served to undermine the revolutionary movement.

During this same period, the RSDWP held its founding congress in a small wooden house in Minsk, Belarus, on 13–15 March 1898, an event of striking insignificance given what was to follow. Virtually all attendees were arrested afterward, no records of the meeting were left, and there appeared to be some doubt whether there would ever be another congress. Certainly it could not be held within the borders of the Russian Empire, where it would be penetrated all too easily by the secret police (Okhrana). In 1900, the Social Democrats established their own newspaper, called *Iskra* (The Spark). But this positive development was soon to be offset by internal rifts. Lenin was to be the key instigator. After his period of exile Lenin returned to western Europe, and once again his chief preoccupation was with the Economists. In 1902 he published his most famous polemical work, *What Is To Be Done?*, the title of which was taken from the pamphlet of his mentor Nikolay Chernyshevsky, though the writing was far more dynamic and divisive than that of his revolutionary predecessor.

What Is To Be Done? reads like a programme for revolutionary action, but it is also a work that reflects Lenin's disillusionment with the chosen class for such action, the proletariat. The traditional Marxist view was deterministic, maintaining that the class conflict was to follow an inevitable pattern, with the bourgeoisie rising up against the feudal aristocracy as a result of the capitalist period, and with a subsequent later struggle between the proletariat against their bourgeois masters. The role of a revolutionary party, it had been surmised by Russian Marxists, was merely to help this process along and wait for the rising of the working class. Lenin, either through impatience or contempt for the proletariat, maintained that left to itself, the latter would do nothing. Hence the Russian Social Democrats must take power on behalf of the workers and rule in their name. To do so the party must be highly centralized, and composed of a small group of ruthless and dedicated revolutionaries. There would be no room in this party for sympathizers of the movement, liberals, or otherwise. According to Adam B. Ulam, this programme was a 'blueprint for a dictatorship' [72]. Robert V. Daniels perceives it as part of Lenin's drive for personal authority [52]. There is no question that this pamphlet proved to be politically the most important of Lenin's writings.

Its appearance was followed closely by the Second Congress of the RSDWP, initially held in Brussels, but later moved to London following its closure by the Belgian police. Among the 57 delegates were the most prominent Social Democrats centred around the *Iskra* newspaper, together with an independent socialist group, the Jewish Bund (League). Lenin reiterated his view that the workers, left to their own devices, were not a revolutionary instrument and that most of them were not even aware of Marx's writings. What was required was a system of 'democratic centralism', whereby the main decisions would be taken by a small party of committed and experienced revolutionaries working through a party central committee, which would be elected by a party congress. His emphasis was on rigid discipline in order to take state power. Such views horrified his contemporaries, including his friend Martov, Plekhanov and the older generation (Pavel Akselrod, Vera Zasulich, and others), and fellow Social Democrat L.D. Trotsky, from the Odessa region. In their view Lenin was advocating the rule of a minority party over the workers that would ultimately result in a dictatorship.

There seemed to be little chance that Lenin's views would prevail, but further arguments during the Congress led to the departure of the Jewish Bund in protest. As a result, Lenin and his followers were left in a small majority and their faction adopted the name Bolsheviks. The Martov faction was then termed the minority, or Mensheviks. For the latter it was one of the misfortunes of their political life, but at the time there seemed little likelihood that the rift would be permanent. The Social Democrats were still pitifully small in numbers and the fact that they were unable to present a united front, even when meeting in exile, did not augur well for the future. Had Lenin changed? Why did a man who in the past had listened to and respected the views of his colleagues suddenly become the advocate of a ruthless dictatorship under strict party discipline? Clearly Lenin felt that Russian revolutionaries had a tendency for endless debate – an accusation he was later to direct at the Mensheviks *per se*. In addition, he had learned during his time in St Petersburg – or so he believed – that the workers did not have a natural inclination toward revolutionary activities. This judgement was shortly to prove spectacularly inaccurate, but it was not the first mistake to be made by Lenin. By 1912, the split in the Russian Social Democratic Workers' Party was to become permanent when the Bolsheviks held a separate conference in Prague.

What gave Lenin his authority over the Bolsheviks? Photographs of him reveal a small, unimposing looking man with a permanently solemn and often severe expression. Highly strung and nervous, his appearance was modest to the point of being shabby. Lenin was a fanatic, and a man of great discipline and willpower. He appears to have had no social or family life outside politics. Rumours have circulated for years that he had a romantic liaison with the French revolutionary Inessa Armand, but if so it must have been a singularly dull affair. Likewise when he came to Petrograd in 1917 and stayed in the apartment of an attractive widow, he had the opportunity for dalliance but there is little evidence that he was concerned about anything other than his political goals. In Soviet works, it was not untypical to read portrayals of Lenin as a man concerned with the plight of the workers of Russia, and the inhumanities and inequities of the capitalist system. However, there is little that is humanitarian in his writing. It is incisive, vindictive, argumentative [12]. Lenin wanted power, he wanted it for his party alone with himself as leader, and he would analyse the political situation and choose the methods by which this might best occur. It seemed unlikely to this most rational of men that this would happen during his lifetime. Nonetheless, this goal seems to have been his main motivation. This is not to say that he was not a Marxist, but he was hardly a passive follower of Marx; rather, he would adapt the doctrine to the political situation of Russia. Economism was attacked with such venom precisely because it threatened to take away from Lenin his dream of revolution in Russia. The quest for power was the driving force behind everything that Lenin did.

RUSSIA'S WAR WITH JAPAN

Russia was experiencing a difficult economic period at the start of the twentieth century and the government of Tsar Nikolay II appeared powerless to do much about it. In 1903 workers' strikes broke out in the oilfields of Baku and spread quickly to other towns in the Caucasus, provoked further by the revolutionary agitation of the RSDWP. In Ukraine there were strikes in the two major industrial cities of Kiev and Odessa. Peasant riots developed into direct assaults on the property of landowners. At this same time

Russia and Japan came into conflict in the Far East. Nikolay II and his Interior Minister Vyacheslav Von Plehve decided that a short war with Japan might enhance the popularity of the government. On the other hand, Japanese aggression gave the Russian government little choice in the matter. But the main question was how best to fight a war so distant from St Petersburg. There were only two possibilities: to make extensive use of the Trans-Siberian Railroad to transport troops and supplies; and to gain control over the sea. The war began in February 1904 and the naive tsar did not expect it to last very long or to end in disaster.

Prior to 1904–5, no Asian power had defeated a European power in battle in recent memory. Consequently the military prowess and commitment of Japan was seriously underestimated by the Russian side. The Japanese quickly brought their fleet into the ocean, trapping the Russian Pacific ships in the harbours of Port Arthur and Chemulpo. The conflict on land was protracted and costly in terms of casualties for both sides. The Russians were pushed back at the battles of Yalu River (1 May 1904) and Liao-Yang (24 August 1904), but they were not defeated. After a further indecisive battle at the Sha-ho River, the Russian land forces retreated. The fleet remained trapped at Port Arthur, and the Japanese sacrificed thousands of lives in an unsuccessful attempt to capture this key strategic port. It was then put to siege. An attempted breakout in August was repulsed with the loss of several Russian ships. Subsequently, the Russian government decided on a remarkable policy: to send the Baltic Fleet under Admiral Z.P. Rozhdestvensky halfway around the world to alleviate the besieged port.

In the meantime two further setbacks befell the Russians. The first was the huge psychological setback of the fall of Port Arthur on 1 January 1905, months before the scheduled arrival of the Baltic Fleet. The second was the defeat of General A.N. Kuropatkin's army at the battle of Mukden in February 1905. The latter was not a particularly decisive defeat, but the Japanese were left in control of the city and it effectively ended the land warfare of the Russo-Japanese War. The Baltic Fleet finally reached the China Sea in May 1905 but had run into serious fuel problems. On its way to the port of Vladivostok to obtain supplies of coal, it ran into a carefully prepared Japanese ambush at what became known as the battle of Tsushima, on 27–28 May 1905, and the result was the spectacular demise of the fleet after a feat of exceptional navigational skill. More than 60 per cent of the fleet's ships were lost and only a handful escaped to Vladivostok. Though the Japanese army was a spent force, the success at sea was the decisive event of the war and sent shock waves through the Russian Empire. The humiliating failure was a severe blow to the regime of Nikolay II.

The war was ended through American mediation by the Treaty of Portsmouth (Maine) in August 1905, and ended Russian ambitions in the

Far East until the end of the Second World War. Most of the gains in East Asia were lost. The Japanese retained Port Arthur, Russian lands of southern Manchuria, Korea (which was overrun by the Japanese even while peace negotiations were under way) and south Sakhalin Island. Japan emerged as a new power in the Far East. The war was significant for the revolutionary movement in that it was an important factor in the events taking place in St Petersburg in 1905. On its own, the war would have lowered the prestige of the government and caused an acute crisis. Frequent mutinies occurred in the army and navy after the defeat in Japan. But a severe economic situation, combined with revolutionary actions and a growing rift between the government and the public, contributed to the upheaval known as the 1905 Revolution, which might have overthrown the state altogether.

THE REVOLUTION OF 1905

While the war was in progress, representatives of the village organs of self-government – the *zemstva* – came to St Petersburg to ask for adequate representation and rights. The *zemstva* had been founded in 1864 and given control over some facets of village life, such as schools and hospitals. This request was rejected and more radical elements came to the fore. The first event of note in 1905 is the most famous: a peaceful march of St Petersburg workers to bring a petition to the tsar, who was thought to be at the Winter Palace (although he was actually absent at the time). The march, on 22 January 1905, was led by Georgy Gapon, a renegade priest with close contacts with the Okhrana, but whom many sources believe to have had a genuine interest in the plight of the urban proletariat in the capital city. Though the slogans carried by the marchers attacked government officials, they were humble in tone in their addresses to the tsar. The workers demanded improved working conditions, lower taxes, and equal treatment under the law – hardly excessive demands [48]. A significant portion of the workers came from the giant Putilov armaments factory, which also produced locomotives.

As the petition approached the Winter Palace, the marchers were fired upon by Cossack troops, commanded by the tsar's uncle, the Grand Duke Vladimir. The numbers killed have never been satisfactorily assessed – they vary between 200 and 1,500 – but without doubt hundreds were injured. The regime had turned on its own workers, and the absent tsar, Nikolay II, was directly associated with this action, which initiated the revolution. It was precisely the factory workers who began the mass protests later in the year. The protests had reached a mass scale by the summer, and Tsar Nikolay II was obliged to agree to reduce his own powers by granting wider popular representation to a parliament in August [*Doc. 1*]. This concession did not stem the revolutionary tide, however, and by October a general strike was in place that crippled the capital. Both the middle classes and the workers participated. Railways came to a halt and all the factories were shut down. The tsar's ministers, led by S. Witte, informed him that further concessions were necessary, and in October the tsar abjectly issued a Manifesto by which the government agreed to both a Constitution and an elected assembly with legal powers (the Duma). A Council of Ministers was formed with Witte as the chief (prime) minister. Nikolay II's nature was strongly against such concessions. Though not an active ruler who took initiatives, the very essence of his rule was to conserve his autocratic powers as he had inherited them from his father. He was forced to take such a 'backward' step because he was isolated in his own capital.

The concessions did not satisfy all parties but they were effective in dividing the revolutionaries [*Doc. 2*]. By this time, the St Petersburg workers had elected their own council, or soviet. Initially it was led by G. Khrustalev-Nosar and subsequently by the Social Democrat (at that time alienated from Lenin) L.D. Trotsky. There were risings in other towns, most seriously in Moscow, where about 1,000 workers were killed in December in clashes with government troops. The Kadets under Pavel Milyukov, a well-known historian, were prepared to continue the protests alongside their (temporary) Marxist allies pending the formation of a Constituent Assembly. However, a substantial group of moderate liberals, led by Dmitry Shipov, professed themselves satisfied by the tsar's moves, and formed a new party, the Octobrists, the goal of which was to ensure that the tsar lived up to the promises he had made on 30 October 1905. A significant portion of the workers were also satiated and returned to their jobs. By the end of the year the revolution had petered out.

Was the 1905 Revolution a failure? Clearly it had failed as a revolution since it did not bring about a change of ruler. It did alter somewhat the way in which Russia was ruled and brought into question the autocratic powers of the tsar. But there was no unity of purpose among the groups that took to the streets in St Petersburg. There was little middle ground between a Milyukov and a Trotsky, or between a Shipov and a Milyukov. The revolution collapsed ultimately because the government's concessions divided the liberals, who were unsure of what exactly they were fighting for and repelled by the excesses and more extreme aims of the socialists. The Social Democrats had not anticipated the upheaval, and of the leading figures in the party, only Trotsky played a brief role in the revolutionary actions. Nonetheless, 1905 was a highly significant event: it led to the formation of a Duma and it saw the initiation of the St Petersburg Soviet, which was to play a pivotal role in 1917. The government, in turn, had suffered a grave shock and would try to recover [41; 42].

Even before the Duma met in May 1906, the government had taken advantage of the more peaceful situation to make some counter-moves.

Chief among these was the issuance of the Fundamental Laws, which could only be altered with the express permission of the tsar. Alongside the Duma would be another body called the State Council, whose members would be chosen from the elite of society: the nobility, church, *zemstva*, and the more successful business circles. The tsar would retain the title of 'autocrat' and would continue to be responsible for foreign policy and declarations of war and peace. Moreover, he would remain the supreme commander of the army and the fleet. He would also have complete control over state finances. Only the tsar could appoint or remove ministers. The Fundamental Laws were intended to be an impediment to the operation of the Duma and the concessions granted during the October days of 1905. The Duma, thus opposed, had no opportunity to become a Constituent Assembly, as the Kadets had wished. Much of the optimism of 1905 had disappeared therefore by the spring of 1906 [42; 45].

THE DUMAS AND STOLYPIN

With the Fundamental Laws in place (and Russia never got a firm Constitution until 1918), elections to the Duma took place, but they were boycotted by most parties of the Far Left. The best organized of the parties taking part was the Kadets, who won 160 out of the 524 seats in the new assembly. Labour supporters – the Trudoviki – won 94 seats; the Social Democrats, represented mainly by Mensheviks from Georgia, obtained 18 seats; the Octobrists received 17; and 15 were taken by parties of the Far Right. From the perspective of the government, the First Duma was hardly congenial in membership, and so it proved in practice. It at once began with demands for the repeal of the Fundamental Laws, a request that could unite all parties other than those of the Far Right. It had been elected by a system of voting that was far from democratic – though far more egalitarian than was to be the case in future elections. Landowners, small peasants, and those with professional occupations in the urban population were permitted to vote; while the military, students, and the clergy were disenfranchised.

On 20 July 1906 the tsar appointed Petr Stolypin as his new Prime Minister of the Cabinet, and the First Duma was promptly dissolved. About one-third of the deputies protested against the dissolution, which had been backed by the threat though not the use of military force, by travelling north to the town of Vyborg and issuing a protest to the population. The renegade deputies demanded that the public should refuse either to pay taxes or to provide military service until the Duma was reconvened. Little attention was paid to these pleas. For much of the population the Duma was a novelty. It was shortly replaced by the Second Duma, a more radical body since the socialist groups decided to participate *en masse*. The result, which saw the previously large Kadet faction severely reduced and the number of socialist deputies considerably increased, was predictable. The Second Duma was dissolved on 16 June 1907, and several troublesome Social Democratic deputies were arrested. The government had clearly recovered from its desperate situation in 1905. The question was whether it could survive without a parliament altogether.

Before a Third Duma was elected, changes were made to the social composition of the electorate. The franchise was altered to ensure that 50 per cent of delegates were elected by wealthy landowners and 14 per cent by urban merchants. Those elected by the peasantry were reduced from 42 to 22 per cent; and the workers could elect only about 2 per cent of delegates. In addition, the representation of non-Russians in the Duma was drastically curtailed. Poles, Georgians, and other groups had proved particularly recalcitrant in the first two Dumas. The Third Duma was a parliament that represented mainly the propertied classes, supported by the new middle classes in the cities. Representation of the Kadets and Social Democrats was meagre. Nevertheless, with the Third Duma a certain compromise was reached between the government and society. It indubitably played a significant role in policy-making and in agriculture. In 1912 when its mandate ended, it was replaced by the Fourth Duma.

Like Witte, Stolypin stands out in contrast to the mediocrities who were given ministerial rank under Nikolay II. In the spring of 1906 he became the Minister of Internal Affairs, and without relinquishing this position he became the Prime Minister in July. A strong personality, he took up his position at a time when the state was groping for policy direction, but importantly when the manifestations of revolutionary activity were at a low ebb. He came to be resented by the high nobility and by the socialists – the phrase 'Stolypin the butcher' was in evidence before long – but he came to be the charismatic leader figure of the Duma and a favourite of the tsar. His main priority was the peasantry. In 1905–6, the fury of the peasants in the countryside had surprised many in the government. Peasant revolts had been a regular feature of Russian life since the eighteenth century, but they were particularly dangerous to the government when combined with the disaffection of the growing urban proletariat. Hopes that the peasants would be pacified by the village community system – the *mir* – had proved unrealistic. In 1905, all remaining redemption dues had been cancelled, but the problem remained how to regain peasant support for the government.

Stolypin's solution was to divide the peasants by creating a stratum of small landowners, thereby withdrawing support for the village community. The peasants could now claim their separate strips of land, which were often scattered miles apart, consolidate them as their personal property, and leave the village community. This land could if necessary be enclosed. The move was called a 'wager on the strong' because it was posited that those who could not make ends meet would sell up their land and move to the cities, while those that remained behind would become small farmers in the western European sense, providing a haven of stability in the countryside without affecting the status of the landowners, who were not anxious to see their own position further eroded by concessions to the peasants [54]. Stolypin's policy came into law on 22 November 1907, at which time an individual peasant could request his share of land in a consolidated holding. The desire to break up the village communities in their entirety was reflected in a law of 10 July 1910, at which time a village community could dissolve itself by a majority vote of the male heads of household.

The Stolypin reform was a qualified success. By the outbreak of war in 1914, over one-third of peasant households had left the village community. A much smaller number had consolidated their holdings and become small farmers, however – perhaps 10 per cent in all of the European part of the Russian Empire. An analogous situation is seen in Russia today when, given the option of leaving the collective farm, many peasants choose to remain because of the security offered by a collective organization. The Stolypin reform required more initiative than the peasants were prepared to show in the period 1907–14. Within two years, the initial enthusiasm for the move had given way to doubts and a significant drop in the number of peasants choosing to leave the community. The assassination of Stolypin in 1911 and, more importantly, the outbreak of war in 1914 precluded in any case the possibility of bringing this reform to fruition. The Social Democrats were somewhat divided on the reform. On the one hand it threatened to bring capitalism to the village, thereby depriving the urban workers of an ally in the revolutionary struggle. On the other hand the onset of rural individual farming could be perceived as following the Marxist pattern of the growth of rural capitalism, that is a progressive move that signalled that Russia was moving in the same direction as the more advanced nations of Europe.

THE ROYAL FAMILY AND RASPUTIN

Nikolay II has received a mixed press from historians. Some perceive him as a good family man who ruled at a time of unprecedented problems, when the Russian Empire collapsed as a result of strains over which he had little control. Others portray him as incompetent, a ruler who presided over a sudden collapse, having inherited a stable state from his father, and a weak man who lacked the ability to follow one policy through to its conclusion. The latter view accords a similar role to his German-born wife, the Tsarina Aleksandra, who was a stronger personality than her husband but whose ideas usually made a situation worse than it had been. In 1913 the dynasty was to celebrate its third century in power with an ostentatious display in the capital. But the Russian Empire was in decline, a decline masked perhaps by the more obvious decline of its counterparts in Turkey and Austria-Hungary. Nikolay II was committed to maintaining the authority with which he had been invested, as the 'tsar of all the Russias'. His was a fitting personality to preside over the collapse of the empire. When he finally departed from the scene in March 1917, the effect was no more than that of a lamp going out [*Doc. 4*].

The royal family was a cause of private concern to the tsar and tsarina. After the birth of four daughters, they had been rewarded with the birth of a son, Aleksey, in 1901, but he was a sickly child and suffered from haemophilia, a disease inherited from the maternal side of the family (ultimately from Queen Victoria) and carefully concealed from the Russian public. The superstitious tsarina tried out a number of dubious healers before the royal family was introduced to the wandering mystic Rasputin in the autumn of 1905. None were able to stop the potentially lethal bleeding when the tsarevich suffered a fall or bump. Rasputin was to fill this role, but he was more than just a 'family doctor', despite his remarkable powers of healing, which cannot be explained by contemporary medicine. Rasputin was perceived as an authentic man of the village with his long dark flowing hair and beard, a genuine representative of the Russian people and its natural goodness, a sinner who had repented and was now welcomed by the upper echelons of the Russian Orthodox Church [32].

Rasputin was a fascinating personality and captured the popular imagination at that time and subsequently. Because of his influence on the tsarina – she always referred to him as 'Our Friend' in her letters to the tsar – he has been accorded a major role in the eventual downfall of the monarchy. This claim has been enhanced by the fact that it was a member of the royal family who engineered his assassination by cyanide poisoning, shooting and finally flogging with chains before being dumped in a Petrograd canal in December 1916. One can respond to this assertion with two statements. First, Rasputin's influence cannot be perceived as totally harmful. In addition to healing Aleksey, he also exposed some of the hypocrisy in the Russian Orthodox Church, and he was one of the few people of influence in ruling circles to come out strongly against participation in the First World War.

Second, Rasputin came to wield political influence in Russia (as opposed to being a warm acquaintance of the royal family) relatively late, at the time of the outbreak of war, or for just three years out of 23 in the reign of Nikolay II. None of the problems that beset Russia can be attributed to Rasputin [28]. Rather he was a symbol of the rift that had developed between the monarch and his subjects. This rift began at the very beginning of Nikolay's reign, when some 1,500 of his subjects were crushed to death at an outdoor ceremony in honour of the royal company, after which Nikolay and Aleksandra attended a reception at the French Embassy as if nothing had happened. The tsarina was never popular, and in August 1914, when Germany and Russia were in a state of war, she was widely regarded as a traitor. Nikolay II suffered further setbacks with the massacre of Bloody Sunday (described above) and the loss of prestige in the military defeat by Japan. The elevation of Rasputin did not bring down the monarchy; it was rather a reflection of the poor choice of counsellors in the latter part of the reign of the last Romanov.

THE FIRST WORLD WAR

The origins of the First World War are complex and involve the politics of all the countries of Europe. The Russian role was determined by two major factors: an alliance with France, and subsequently with Britain, which pitted Russia against Germany, a power that was seeking to play a greater role in world politics since its unification in 1871; and support for the claims of fellow Slavs, particularly the Serbs, within the Austro-Hungarian Empire and in Serbia itself. In turn, the Austrians were anxious to crush completely any manifestations of rebellion in their multi-national empire in the justifiable belief that it would have a domino effect on many other territories. Paradoxically most of the heads of the ruling monarchies – Germany, Britain, Russia – were closely related. It seemed inconceivable to Nikolay II that he could be at war with the country of his cousin, Kaiser Wilhelm II of Germany. Another cousin, George V of England, played a less influential role in politics.

Russian participation in the war owed much to Germany and German military thinking. This was based on the Schlieffen Plan, finalized in 1905, and modifications thereof. The Germans believed that if war broke out, it would be impossible for them to fight a war on two fronts against France and Russia. Since the Russians would take, it was believed, about six weeks to mobilize their cumbersome, though formidably large army, it would be necessary to strike a devastating blow at France before wheeling their armies to the Eastern Front against Russia. The war in western Europe, then, in the German view, had to be ended in six weeks. For the Russians the dilemma was similar. It was considered essential in the event of war that the Russians should mobilize their army before those of their adversaries, otherwise there was a conceivable danger of Russia being overrun before the country was properly prepared.

Because the war proved to be a decisive event in the collapse of the Romanov dynasty, its origins perhaps merit a closer observation. Unfortunately these reveal little in terms of Russian planning or foresight. The European alliance system was a case in point. In 1894 Russia had signed a secret military alliance with France, directed ostensibly against Britain, Russia's great rival in South Asia. But in 1904 Britain and France signed an

Entente Cordiale in order to divide up the spoils in North Africa. After the defeat by Japan in 1905, Russia no longer appeared a threat to the British, while the Russians were eager to add British investment to that of France and Germany in the developing Russian industrial complex. The two imperialist powers divided up Persia into spheres of respective influence (the Russians in the north, the British in the south), while Russia pulled her troops out of Afghanistan. The Triple Entente was now in place and was to prove both durable and a commitment from which it was exceptionally difficult for the Russians to break free when the course of war turned sour on them.

In October 1908, tension in the Balkans mounted when the Austro-Hungarian Empire annexed the province of Bosnia-Herzegovina from the Turks, a move that was widely perceived as affecting the interests of neighbouring Serbia. The Austrian action also had the approval of its German ally. Approximately 3 million Serbs lived in Bosnia-Herzegovina and Serbia appealed for Russian aid. The Russians suggested to the British and French that an international conference be held to resolve the situation (a similar undertaking had resolved a crisis in Morocco in January 1906), but the French proved unwilling to take such a step in view of Germany's unqualified support of its Austrian allies. Russia had thus been humiliated in diplomatic terms and began to increase its military buildup. The situation in the Balkans was proving to be precarious since the old Ottoman Empire no longer had the power to keep the subject nations in check. In 1912, with Russian backing, Bulgaria, Serbia, Montenegro and Greece formed a Balkan League, which promptly declared war on Turkey.

The Balkan Wars of 1912 and 1913 resulted in the complete defeat of Turkey by the league and in British mediation at a peace treaty in London in May 1913, which divided up the Turks' former territories on the European continent. Though the war had been conducted successfully, the Treaty of London was also perceived in St Petersburg as disastrous. Serbia had insisted on its annexation of Albania, but the Germans – surprisingly supported by the British – agreed that Albania should become independent. On two occasions, then, Russia had appeared to let down its Serbian ally. A second Balkan war soon broke out between Bulgaria and Serbia over the spoils of the London treaty, however, and this time the Serbs did gain significant territory from Bulgaria and Macedonia. This consequence had the unfortunate repercussion of emboldening the Serbs to seek more gains, and to foment trouble among their compatriots in the Austro-Hungarian Empire. This move occurred precisely at a time when the Russians were determined not to let down their Serbian ally when they were next put to the test diplomatically.

The spark for the First World War was the assassination of Franz Ferdinand, archduke and the heir to the Austro-Hungarian throne as the nephew of Emperor Franz-Josef, while on a visit to Sarajevo, Bosnia. The assassination was the work of a member of the Black Hand, a Serbian terrorist group, and not the Serbian government, although the latter was implicated indirectly. The decision to punish Serbia appears to have been made not by the emperor personally, but by his chief of staff, Konrad Von Hoetzendorff, who felt that a quick and victorious war would reverse the gains made recently by the Serbs and stabilize the situation in the empire. With the complete support of Germany, the Austrians sent the Serbs an ultimatum which basically undermined the entire concept of Serbian sovereignty on 23 July 1914. The Russians now faced a serious dilemma and on 25 July a preliminary mobilization of the army was ordered. At the same time, Nikolay II was sending telegrams to Kaiser Wilhelm II to try to find a way out of the impasse. Initially a ridiculous solution was proposed by the tsar, namely to order a mobilization against Austria-Hungary, but not against Germany. Only after the frantic persuasion of his generals did Nikolay order a full mobilization against the two powers.

Once Russia mobilized then the Germans were obliged, by their own thinking, to put the Schlieffen Plan into operation. In St Petersburg, though the tsar genuinely tried to avoid war, there was no premonition of disaster. On the contrary, as in the other European capitals, there was genuine enthusiasm for war, which was not anticipated to be a protracted affair. A war against Germany might even serve some interests of Russia as both Bulgaria and Turkey were falling increasingly under German influence. The role of Russia's old enemy, Turkey, was paramount. As long as Turkey remained outside the conflict and the Dardanelles remained open, the French and British navies had a passage to the Black Sea in order to bring supplies to Russia. In turn, the great value of Russia to its allies was manpower. The Russian army, by its sheer size, was a formidable force and it was getting stronger by the year. The Germans recognized this. From the German perspective a war against Russia was preferable in 1914 rather than in 1916.

War proved initially a great rallying cry for the government. Very few Duma deputies opposed it. The Trudoviki, for example, supported it, as did the Kadets and even prominent Marxists such as Georgii Plekhanov, who saw a greater danger in German militarism than in succumbing to the wishes of imperialist governments. Some socialists wanted a peace treaty without territorial changes or indemnities, but were prepared to begin war while such negotiations took place. Lenin, the Bolshevik leader, was living abroad, and few heeded his cry that an imperialist war should be transformed into a civil war, i.e. that it was in the revolutionaries' interest that Russia should suffer defeat. His views were eventually published in his polemic *Imperialism: The Highest Stage of Capitalism* in 1916. But what appears in retrospect to be gross naivety also occurred in other capitals. Lenin was horrified to learn that the German Social Democrats had also given their support to the German war effort. In August 1914, the revolutionary movements of Europe appeared to be at a very low ebb. But appearances were misleading because war has always been the great catalyst of revolution and change. The First World War was a cataclysm like none before it.

Russian mobilization occurred much faster than predicted even by the most pessimistic of German military planners. Initially some 1.5 million troops were mobilized, with a further 5 million in reserve. The Russian army had use of 60 batteries of artillery and was divided into several fronts. The two main ones were the North-West, directed against the German territory of East Prussia; and the South-West, directed against Austria-Hungary through a territory composed mainly of ethnic minorities who might be expected to show some sympathy toward an invading Russian army. A third army was in the Caucasus guarding that territory against any possible Turkish encroachments (though Turkey was not yet in the war). A fourth was in the south of Ukraine, based at Odessa. A fifth was on the Baltic coast. It was the first two armies that were called to action quickly, as the desperate French appealed to their Russian ally for a diversionary action to take pressure off their troops in western Europe. The failure of the Schlieffen Plan was soon evident, and the Germans were obliged to respond to the Russian invasion of East Prussia.

The Russian army was not fully prepared for war in August 1914, though the situation was not as desperate as sometimes portrayed. Two great armies invaded East Prussia: the First Army under General Paul Rennenkampf on the Niemen; and the Second Army under General Aleksandr Samsonov, which moved northward from Poland. Though German forces were weak, the Russians were badly led. The two commanders barely communicated with each other. Samsonov had little idea where he was once he entered German territory, and the Russian commanders communicated by open radio, so that the Germans could ascertain their exact whereabouts. As a result, the Germans were able to keep the two great Russian armies separated and fight each in turn: Samsonov was overwhelmed at the battle of Tannenberg (27–30 August 1914) by General Von Francois, one of the greatest defeats in Russian military history. Samsonov suffered 125,000 casualties and committed suicide afterward. Rennenkampf, who had seemed extraordinarily reticent about engaging the Germans, promptly ordered a general retreat when he encountered Von Francois's army, despite the fact that it had just marched 120 kilometres in four days and might have been a weakened force. On 4 September the two armies clashed at Masurian Lakes, and about 45,000 Russian prisoners were taken. Rennenkampf at least managed to preserve the bulk of his army.

These two battles were probably the most decisive in Russia's war effort. They revealed the superiority of German military strategy, led by

Field Marshal Paul Von Hindenburg on the Eastern Front. The Russians were never able to penetrate German territory again in the war. In the south-west, matters were quite different because the army of the Austro-Hungarian Empire was both smaller and weaker than its Russian counterpart. By 3 September, the Russians had reached and captured the city of L'viv (L'vov, Lemberg). But on 31 October, Turkey entered the war. Its action and the control over the Baltic Sea by the German Fleet effectively cut Russia off from its allies in the west. For the remainder of the war, Russia fought alone, increasingly short of materiel and weapons, and with a faulty supply line that was never fully remedied. In the major cities there were long lines outside bread shops and rations were increasingly reduced. The long war began to take an acute toll on the Russian population.

The lack of success continued in 1915 after the Germans mounted a major attack on Russia's Polish territories in the spring. Most of Poland soon fell into German hands, and Russian casualties were enormous, around a million. It was necessary to step up recruitment and the Russian army became basically a peasant one, composed of raw recruits. It was not unusual for these peasants to go into battle without a rifle. The hope was that they would retrieve weapons from their adversaries during the course of a battle. The army took on the appearance of a swollen mass of new recruits, disillusioned by the constant defeats. The one succour had been the respect of the army for its Commander-in-Chief, the Grand Duke Nikolay, uncle of the tsar, an imposing figure who inspired confidence by his very appearance. However, at the behest of his wife, the tsar decided to take personal command of his armies on 22 August 1915. Military headquarters by that time were in the Belarusian town of Mogilev.

The tsar thus left his capital at a critical juncture and henceforth the Russian government and appointments of key figures were in the hands of the unpopular and hapless tsarina, a woman who felt that the members of the Fourth Duma – led by a majority of deputies who had formed a Progressive Bloc – should be excluded entirely from a role in decision-making. Shortly thereafter most of the able (and more liberal) ministers in the government were removed by the tsarina, often at the behest of Rasputin. They included Prince N.B. Shcherbatov, Minister of the Interior, A.V. Krivoshein, Minister of Agriculture, General A.A. Polivanov, Minister of War, and Foreign Minister S.D. Sazonov, all in the period between January and June 1916. Prime Minister I.L. Goremykin, who had refused to add his name to those opposing Nikolay's leadership of the armies, was also dismissed in January 1916 and replaced by the bumbling and ineffectual Boris Sturmer [21]. Perhaps the single most unpopular figure was the new Minister of the Interior, Aleksandr Protopopov. The quality level of the Russian government was critically reduced therefore in the early months of 1916.

It should be noted that the First World War was very costly to all the great powers of Europe. Never before had so many men been sacrificed for so little territorial gain. Even powers that were eventually victorious, such as France, suffered mutinies in their armies. The trench warfare in western Europe was as catastrophic as the more mobile warfare on the Eastern Front. On the whole, however, the European armies proved to be more disciplined, particularly the Germans. In Russia, the mass conscription had also left vast areas of land uncultivated. Grain production had fallen by half by 1916. Even in the summer of 1915, strikes and food riots broke out in Moscow. A similarly tense situation arose in Petrograd (the Russified version of the name given to the capital at the outbreak of war with Germany: St Petersburg, a name of Dutch derivation, sounded too German to Russian ears).

The Russian government was in a critical dilemma. Committed to the alliance with France and Britain, it proved to be a demonstrably loyal ally. But the country was not prepared for a long war, nor could it supply adequately the mass swollen army that was in the field by 1916. Against the Austrians alone, Russia might have been capable of success, but the Germans regularly came to the aid of their ally. The question that many asked was what was the aim of the war. By 1916 it had become unclear. In terms of casualties Russians had made the greatest sacrifices. Poland was now wholly in the hands of the Germans and other territories of the European part of the empire were threatened. Nikolay II was an ineffectual and uninspiring leader of men. There was effectively no government in St Petersburg. The increasing economic hardship and the succession of military defeats deprived the government of any credibility it had maintained. At the same time the monarchy was woefully oblivious to the danger that had arisen. It had learned little from the experience of 1905 and proved unwilling to appoint a more representative Cabinet or to work with the Duma. The country was ripe for an upheaval.

PART TWO   REVOLUTION AND WAR

CHAPTER TWO

THE MARCH REVOLUTION

THE FIRST DAYS

The outbreak of revolution in Petrograd in March 1917 (February, O.S.) was initially an isolated affair. As Trotsky has remarked, the capital alone was responsible for the revolution, and the rest of the country was obliged to follow [18]. The city possessed 1.3 per cent of the population of Russia, in its territorial form at the outbreak of war. Older sources have described the revolution as 'spontaneous' and 'leaderless' [5], but this is not a broadly accepted view today [59]. It can be said that the initial intention of those who took to the streets on 8 March was hardly to overthrow the monarchy. But once the masses had taken to the streets, there were groups within them that actively pursued the downfall of the old regime. The March Revolution – a name that we will use throughout, even though by the Julian calendar used in Russia it took place in February – was a massive and successful social revolution. But it began merely as a protest against existing conditions.

On 8 March female workers of the Vyborg district of Petrograd commemorated International Women's Day while at the same time using the occasion to demand bread. On this day also a new food rationing system was introduced by the government. A strike was declared in the textile mills and virtually all the Vyborg factories were closed down. Combined with metalworkers, the number of strikers is estimated to have been between 78,000 and 80,000 on the first day of activity. The key factor was to be the reaction of the 160,000-strong Petrograd garrison under the command of General S. Khabalov. Though separated from the front and the orders of the Minister of War, General Mikhail Belyaev, the Petrograd garrison would await the orders of the tsar before restoring order in the capital. As the general waited, the number of strikers increased substantially.

On the second day of protests, 9 March, the number of strikers was approximately double that of the previous day, between 150,000 and 200,000. Though the police carefully guarded bridges over the river, the actual task of dispersing the crowds was left to Cossack troops, who carried out their duties with a notable apathy and disinterest. The masses could thus draw a distinction between these two forces of the authorities. The third day saw a repeat of the critical moment of 1905 when a general strike was announced. Clashes with the police became more serious. With the strike, Petrograd came to a standstill. Banks, schools and restaurants were closed, and all public transport stopped. According to some accounts, the city was approaching anarchy as the police appeared to have lost control. There were several instances of looting and assaults on police officers. The protestors had taken over much of the centre of the city. At this point, the tsar decided to take action, though it is not evident that he considered the situation particularly serious. General Khabalov received the critical order to disperse the demonstrators and to use force if they refused to leave the streets.

The role of the Fourth Duma was negligible because it had come to the end of its term and it was dissolved by Premier Prince N.D. Golitsyn (he had replaced Sturmer in late November 1916), on the orders of the tsar, on 10 March. Nikolay showed no interest in its prompt reconvocation despite frequent admonitions and requests by its leader, a monarchist, Mikhail Rodzianko. The latter sent a series of petitions to the tsar that were treated with contempt. Rodzianko believed that without a new government and prime minister there was no way for the country to emerge from the current crisis. But the tsar simply let the crisis reach its culmination point. On 11 March there seemed initially some cause for optimism. On several occasions the troops had fired on demonstrators and some local Bolsheviks – from the rank and file rather than the leadership – were rounded up. But overnight, the troops began to mutiny, starting with the Volhynian Regiment, and refused to fire further upon their brethren. Gradually the militia of the Petrograd garrison made common cause with the demonstrating workers, isolating the police, who were to become the main victims of the revolution.

By 12 March, the city had fallen into the hands of the revolutionaries. The socialist groups in the capital played an important, if not a pivotal part in events. Deprived of their leadership, those Bolsheviks on the scene cooperated with Mensheviks and Social Revolutionaries, in addition to the so-called Interdistrict group (with which the absent Trotsky was associated), in the protests. But there is no indication that any of these groups, or the workers, soldiers and sailors on the streets, had a clear idea of what the final goal was to be. The tsar in Mogilev decided belatedly to suppress the rebellion. He dismissed Khabalov, who had retreated with what few loyal troops remained to the Winter Palace and was bemused by the events, and dispatched troops under General N.I. Ivanov, who was to replace Khabalov. Ivanov, like his master, seems to have been completely unaware of the magnitude of his task. Nikolay II meanwhile decided that his place was with his family and set off by train for his summer residence at Tsarskoe Selo where the tsarina awaited him. But the line was blocked by revolutionary troops and after a detour the tsar arrived instead at the ancient town of Pskov, the headquarters of the Northern Front, where he carried out his last official duties.

Ivanov's army never arrived in Petrograd. At some point he decided to halt his army following negotiations with Rodzianko, the Duma president. Rodzianko was one of the most frenetic (and literally the largest) actors of these days. His goal was to form a new government that would preserve the monarchy and ensure the welfare of the propertied classes. As a landowner himself, this was in his best interests. He had become aware, however, that the few concessions that Nikolay was prepared to make were not enough to satisfy the crowd. He informed the military commanders that the only conceivable step was for the tsar to resign in favour of his son. Apprised of this information and receiving no dissenting views among his own generals, Nikolay abdicated on 15 March, initially in favour of his son Aleksey. Upon realizing that he would inevitably lose contact with his son under these circumstances since it was anticipated he would be exiled from Russia, and possibly with the boy's lamentable medical history in mind, he abdicated a second time later in the same day in favour of his brother, the Grand Duke Mikhail [*Doc. 4*].

The abdication was conveyed to two emissaries from the former Duma, the Octobrist Party leader, Aleksandr Guchkov, and the leader of the Nationalist group, Vasily Shulgin. They were satisfied with the decision of the tsar to abdicate in favour of his brother, but there were some problems with this decision. First, constitutionally the tsar could offer the Crown only to his offspring, not to other members of his family. Second, when the Duma representatives announced the decision to the local workers of Pskov there were angry protests and it became plain that the workers preferred an end to the monarchy. The Grand Duke refused to accept the throne [27], and in this anti-climatic manner the 300 years of Romanov rule came to an end. From all accounts Nikolay II accepted the situation with quiet decorum and without any outward signs of emotion. The tsarina, informed of the news while at Tsarskoe Selo, was said to be distraught, remarking that her husband had refused to compromise the principles by which he had ruled. Richard Pipes believes that Nikolay's abdication was a result not of the strikes in Petrograd, but of his sense of patriotic duty. He gave way not to the rebels, but to his own generals and ministers [68]. If this is true it only serves to demonstrate the rift between Nikolay II and the populace of his capital city. The two events moreover were clearly related. No one was in favour of a continuation of the monarchy and the only question was with what to replace it.

THE SYSTEM OF DUAL GOVERNMENT

When the tsar had refused to countenance a new government, some members of the dissolved Duma had remained at their posts. Eventually a Duma Temporary Committee was established on 12 March. The former Duma acknowledged that its actions were unofficial by moving from its usual meeting room in the Tauride Palace to another. Also on 12 March, the Petrograd Soviet resurfaced, initially calling itself the Petrograd Soviet of Workers' Deputies, and later adding Soldiers to that appellation. The Soviet, both in composition and political leaning, was much closer to the views on the street. Its 250 members represented factories, troops, trade unionists, and Social Democratic deputies of the old Duma, and elected themselves a Temporary Executive Committee of 15 members, none of whom were well known to the public. The Soviet also met in the Tauride Palace and it seemed initially that it might take power. That it could have done so is hardly in doubt, particularly with the revolutionary crowd behind it.

The revolutionary element in the Soviet, however, had to make a judgement about the situation. Its majority was comprised of Social Revolutionaries and Mensheviks. The SRs usually deferred to the Mensheviks on matters of doctrine and thus abided by the latter's interpretation that March 1917 had been, in Marxist terminology, a bourgeois revolution overthrowing the old feudal order. The essential task now was to preserve the gains of the revolution and prevent a return of the old order or counter-revolutionary forces. The forces of the Northern Front were known to be sending troops to the capital to overturn the revolution. Ministers and officials of the tsarist regime had to be rounded up, and the former police forces had to be detained. Thus the role of the Soviet had to be a secondary one: the preservation of the revolution and temporary support of the new government of Russia, a bourgeois government represented by the existing parties and members of the old Duma.

The attitude of the Provisional Government was that stability and order had to be returned to Russia. It represented the landowning aristocracy, the intelligentsia and business circles, rather than the workers, peasants and soldiers. It was provisional in the sense that it had not been elected, and because it would eventually be replaced by a Constituent Assembly that would resolve the most critical issues, including the question of landowner-ship and the division of landlords' estates among the peasants. Representatives of the Octobrists, Kadets and Nationalists initially played the leading roles. A leading Zemstvo figure and Kadet, Prince G.E. Lvov, became the Prime Minister, a compromise candidate, but a widely respected figure from the more progressive wing of the Russian aristocracy. The leader of the Kadets, the historian Pavel Milyukov, took the post of Foreign Minister, and was at once a dominant figure in the Cabinet. One of his allies was the Minister of War and the Navy, Aleksandr Guchkov, who had already played a key role in effecting the abdication of the tsar. A wealthy young magnate from the Ukrainian sugar beet industry, Mykhailo Tereshchenko, was appointed Minister of Finance.

There had been general agreement among the leaders of the Soviet that their members would refrain from joining the government. Two were asked to do so: the Georgian Nikolay Chkeidze, who was offered the post of Minister of Labour; and Aleksandr Kerensky, a flamboyant lawyer and moderate SR, who was offered the position of Minister of Justice. The former, acting on instructions of the Soviet Executive Committee, refused. The latter, following his inner intuition that he was a man of destiny, accepted [11]. Kerensky was thus the first to occupy leading positions in both instruments of dual power. Initially he was very popular and made some fiery speeches that seemed to fit well with the exhilaration of the hour. Russia was in a state of euphoria [*Doc. 3*]. The monarchy was formally abolished by a decree of the old Duma even before the Provisional Government was formed. Moscow had fallen into the hands of the insurgents by 14 March, while the most militant supporters of the change of regime were the sailors in their bases at Kronstadt and Helsinki. The attempts to put down the rising all resulted in failure because the armies mutinied and would not fight against the revolutionary masses. The death penalty for desertion was abolished. But there was still much confusion as to the actual seat of power, and this was never more evident than in the disarray of the mutinous army.

On 14 March, the Petrograd Soviet issued a decree called Order No. 1, which fundamentally changed the nature of the Russian army. One of the great fears of members of the Petrograd garrison was that they would be sent to the front. But this decree revoked the authority of officers over the men, and abolished saluting, standing to attention, and titles for officers. All decisions were to be in the hands of committees of soldiers and sailors, while all military units agreed to follow the orders of the Petrograd Soviet, rather than those of the Provisional Government. The latter was thus not in control over the military in its own capital. Order No. 1 was published in the newspaper of the Petrograd Soviet, *Izvestiya* [52]. One week after its appearance, soldiers swelled the membership of the Soviet to over 3,000. It was a raucous and unwieldy group which relied on its Executive Committee, chaired by Chkeidze, to take any meaningful decisions.

Order No. 1 should have served as a warning to the government that its chief problem was the continuation of the fighting on the Eastern Front. At first, however, it announced its intention to make Russia the most democratic country in the world. All political prisoners were to be freed; regional government was to be elected according to universal suffrage by secret ballot; there was to be no discrimination based on race or property and all civil liberties were to be upheld. Matters of more immediate concern, such as continued participation in the war or the land question, were to be resolved by the Constituent Assembly, the exact date of which was to be decided. In short, then, a government that lacked popular support was prepared to embrace the euphoria of the revolution but not to take steps to resolve two of the critical issues that had led to that revolution in the first place. It thus exacerbated its own weakness and lived up to its name: it could not be more than a temporary phenomenon.

THE RETURN OF LENIN

Lenin was in Zurich at the time of the revolution in Petrograd and was one of the last Bolshevik leaders, together with Zinoviev, to return to the capital. Exiles, such as I.V. Stalin and V.M. Molotov, soon returned from Siberia and took over the newspaper *Pravda* from the lower-ranking Bolsheviks already in Petrograd. As already noted, the Bolsheviks had supported the March Revolution together with members of the other socialist parties. Their inclination was to continue this cooperation, which implied that in contrast to the situation in 1903, the Bolsheviks might after all be prepared to work with the other parties. The bookish L.B. Kamenev overtly agreed with the Menshevik view that the socialist parties should take on the role of a peaceful opposition: maintaining the Provisional Government in power even while opposing some of its policies. The time was not opportune for the socialists to take action despite the popularity of the Soviet. The teachings of Marx had not specified how long the period of bourgeois rule would last, but it seemed quite plain that it would of necessity be a lengthy period.

The Bolshevik leader could do little about such 'errant' policies until he returned home. But the journey was far from simple since the territory in between Switzerland and Russia was occupied by armies hostile to those of the latter country. The German High Command, through an intermediary, heard about Lenin's desire to return home and considered it an astute move that would further impede the Russian war effort. Though his return at the behest of the Germans was to cause some unfortunate repercussions for Lenin in the summer of 1917, it is difficult to see what alternatives he had. Thus Lenin, Krupskaya, Zinoviev and a number of other prominent Bolsheviks were transported across enemy territory in a sealed train, i.e. one that had extra-territorial status. According to the Soviet version of events (1977), all except Lenin were travelling 'incognito' [57], though the German authorities certainly knew whom they were transporting. The train took the group to the port of Sasnitz where they boarded a Swedish freighter across the Baltic Sea to Sweden, reaching Stockholm on 13 April. By 16 April they had reached Tornio, a settlement on the border between

Sweden and Finland, and a train took them to Petrograd and a legendary arrival at the Finland Station later this same day. The station is located directly opposite the Tauride Palace across the water. It was thus a simple matter for members of the Soviet to greet Lenin upon his arrival.

Virtually all socialist groups welcomed the return of Lenin. Kerensky, whose father had been the headmaster of Lenin's school in Simbirsk, had declared from the creation of the dual power that he intended to bring all the Bolshevik exiles home 'with honour'. Chkeidze, as chairman of the Soviet Executive Committee, was on hand to greet Lenin with a bouquet of flowers. Lenin, however, had already earmarked his course of action and by all accounts paid little attention to the non-Bolsheviks. He chided, albeit in a friendly fashion, Kamenev and others for their articles conciliatory to the other parties published in *Pravda*. On the following day, at a meeting of the Bolshevik Central Committee, Lenin astounded his colleagues with a series of proposals that became known as the April Theses (some of the principles were later included in his speech 'On the tasks of the proletariat in the present revolution'). As with his book *What Is To Be Done?* and the Second Congress of the RSDWP, Lenin immediately distanced himself from the other socialist parties, and initially from his own colleagues.

The April Theses sounded initially like the ravings of a madman. Lenin declared that there must be no compromises with the Provisional Government. Instead, Bolsheviks should embrace the slogan 'All power to the soviets!' and work for the overthrow of the government. The war in Europe had to be transformed into a civil war. The police and the army had to be abolished. Land should be socialized and all private lands confiscated. Private banks should be dissolved and replaced by a single national bank under the control of the Petrograd Soviet [*Doc. 5*]. All these demands seemed to demonstrate that Lenin was out of touch with the mood in the capital. On the following day, the Bolshevik Central Committee rejected the Theses by 13 votes to 2. Plekhanov declared them to be 'nonsense', and Kamenev criticized them in detail on the pages of *Pravda*. Temporarily, Lenin, by far the senior figure in his party, seemed to have lost control over the Bolshevik leadership.

Over the next three weeks Lenin worked arduously to change the minds of his fellow Bolsheviks in the knowledge that at the end of this period there was to be an all-Russian Bolshevik conference in Petrograd. His methods were persuasion and even harassment. Lenin's was a far stronger personality than men such as Kamenev and by the time of the conference he was firmly back in charge of his party. The April Theses were accepted by an overwhelming majority at the conference. The stumbling block about the goals contained in the Theses was that the Bolshevik members made up only a small minority of members of the Petrograd Soviet, which was dominated by the Mensheviks and Social Revolutionaries.

Members of both those parties were committed to a temporary alliance with the government. In addition, there was the problem of the calling of the Constituent Assembly, a demand that the Bolsheviks would support consistently throughout 1917. If the new Russian government with a permanent status was to be elected by this assembly, then surely power would be vested in its membership rather than that of the Petrograd Soviet. It would be some time before Lenin could resolve this contradiction.

On 17 May, L.D. Trotsky returned from his exile in New York, having been delayed in transit by the Canadian authorities in Halifax, Nova Scotia [19]. Since the split of 1903, Trotsky had remained on good terms with the Mensheviks while leading his own party, the Interdistrict Group. He embraced a theory of permanent revolution, maintaining that Russia itself could not alone forge a revolutionary path. The revolution must occur in Europe as a whole. Trotsky favoured an armed uprising in Russia, believing that it was not necessary for Russia to be a fully-fledged capitalist state before moving to a socialist revolution. Upon his return to Petrograd he made common cause with Lenin, whom he believed had now adopted his views. The Interdistrict Group contained a number of talented people, such as Vladimir Antonov-Ovseenko, who was to play a key role in the capture of the Winter Palace, and Moisey Uritsky, who later headed the secret police in Petrograd. The Interdistrict Group also had close contacts with members of the Petrograd garrison. The alliance with Trotsky and his faction provided a tremendous boost to Lenin and his followers.

Trotsky did not formally join the Bolshevik Party until August, a fact that was to see him derided as an opportunist latecomer in the disputes of the early 1920s. His mission was first to persuade as many of his own party as possible to join him in moving over to the Bolsheviks. Trotsky, a renowned orator, almost foppish in dress, and arrogant to an extreme, had been the Chairman of the Petrograd Soviet in its final days during the 1905 Revolution. He had little trouble getting himself re-elected to this body. Alongside Trotsky, Lenin had other followers that he could count on for their devotion and loyalty: these included Aleksandra Kollontay, the feminist revolutionary (discussed below); I.V. Stalin, whom Lenin had first met in 1912 and persuaded to work on the question of non-Russians within the empire; and Yakob Sverdlov, who was perhaps the most able and efficient administrator in the Bolshevik Party apparatus and looked so similar to Trotsky that they are often mistaken for each other in photographs of the period. Zinoviev was also one of Lenin's closest associates until the autumn of 1917. His views on the timing of the armed uprising and even its validity were to separate him from his leader on the eve of October.

Thus between April and early June 1917, Lenin's party had suffered an initial internal dispute but ultimately Lenin's will prevailed. The party was strengthened by the alliance between Lenin and Trotsky – there was no question that Lenin was the dominant figure of the two, but there was also no doubt that Trotsky had more rapport with the military, with the Petrograd Soviet, and was a superior orator. Lenin's policies presupposed that the nature of the Soviet would change and its membership would veer to the Left. This anticipation on Lenin's part was based on his knowledge of leading Mensheviks, whom, he believed correctly, would immerse themselves in endless debate. It was also not difficult for Lenin to see that the Provisional Government was in many ways distanced from those who wished to take the revolution further. The government had no popular backing, was led by an aristocrat, and was notably dilatory in dealing with the main problem of the day: that of Russia's continuation in the war and fulfilment of her duties as a reliable ally of Britain and France.

THE PROVISIONAL GOVERNMENT, APRIL–JUNE 1917

The Provisional Government was initially under the sway of Foreign Minister Milyukov, a man whose remarkable erudition was matched by an almost total lack of political acumen. For some time, the government had adhered to a Declaration of War Aims that had been heavily influenced by the Soviet leaders. Russia wished to leave the war without territorial annexations, losses or indemnities. The British and the French, however, made plain to Milyukov their dissatisfaction with this Declaration. Publicly, Milyukov adhered to the official government position, but on 1 May he sent a note by telegram to Paris and London, in which he stated that Russia remained bound by the treaties signed by Tsar Nikolay II in 1915; in short, Russia intended to fight the war to a successful conclusion, the defeat of Germany and its allies, and presumably in Russia's case with territorial expansion at the expense of Turkey.

The telegram was hardly secret. The telegraph officers in Petrograd were Mensheviks and within a very short time members of the Petrograd Soviet were provided with the text of the message [36]. Mass demonstrations took place against both Milyukov and his ally, War Minister Guchkov. The protests took on an anti-government dimension, and the Bolshevik Central Committee and its military organization joined in. The Bolsheviks had been prominent during the May Day demonstrations. Now they seemed to be taking an active anti-government position and there were some serious skirmishes in the streets of the capital, none of which were authorized or approved by Lenin, who seemed unusually cautious once he had the full support of his party. The outcome was the resignation of Milyukov and Guchkov on 4 May. Milyukov was replaced by Tereshchenko, a man whose original entry into the Cabinet had been greeted with hoots of derision by the crowd, none of whom had heard of him hitherto; while Guchkov's replacement was Kerensky, who thereafter was to play the leading role in the government. In addition, five more members of the Petrograd Soviet, all Mensheviks or Social Revolutionaries, joined the Cabinet, including the SR leader, Viktor Chernov, and Irakli Tsereteli of the Mensheviks.

On 16 June the First All-Russian Congress of Soviets gathered in Petrograd with 1,090 delegates. Dominated by Mensheviks and Social Revolutionaries (248 and 285 delegates respectively), the Congress gave tacit approval to the idea of a military offensive under certain conditions. The leadership was convinced that it was necessary to work with the government since there was no other party in Russia that was willing to take power. From his seat Lenin was heard to cry, 'There is'. But his group were in no position to dictate policy. For the moment there appeared to be unity between the war aims of Lvov, Kerensky and the socialist members of the Cabinet. The Bolsheviks constituted less than 10 per cent of the Congress delegates. Their support was clearly growing but the party remained in a small minority within the Soviet Executive Committee.

While the Congress was taking place, workers and soldiers began to gather in Petrograd, demanding that the Congress should take power. The Bolshevik leaders proposed a demonstration on 23 June, but the Congress majority passed a resolution that it should not take place. In the knowledge that they were in no position to take or maintain power, the leaders of the Bolshevik Central Committee cancelled the demonstration the evening before it was due to occur. However, this did little to reduce the numbers on the streets. Both the government and the Soviet Executive Committee feared that the Bolsheviks were planning to seize power. It was resolved that there would indeed be an official demonstration after all. It would be held on 1 July and in the event more than a million people took part, most of them ostensibly in support of the Bolshevik slogans such as 'All power to the soviets!' and 'Peace without annexations!'

On 1 July Kerensky ordered a new Russian offensive in Galicia, and for 12 days the reports were of nothing but success. The Russian army encountered little opposition from the retreating Austrians and the government could make appropriate comparisons with the French revolutionary army's successes at the end of the eighteenth century. But the offensive had moved faster than the supply lines and came to an abrupt halt. The Germans rallied to the defence of the Austrians, and on 19 July the Central Powers pushed through the Russian lines, as the Russian troops dropped their weapons and deserted *en masse*. It was at this juncture that Kerensky restored the death penalty at the front. Most significantly, another military débâcle had occurred and this time a government associated with the Kadets, Social Revolutionaries and Mensheviks was involved. Only the Bolsheviks had made known their opposition both to the offensive and the continuation of the war, a fact that was to change radically the political alignment of the masses, particularly peasant-soldiers, many of whom had supported the SRs previously.

THE JULY DAYS

The July Days deserve a place in the revolutionary chronology of 1917. In scope and in terms of numbers involved, they exceeded those of November and are comparable to those of March. July, however, was a failed uprising, and it has provoked much discussion among scholars. Its causes are unclear. Certainly there were more than one. The initial impetus appears to have been the failure of the Kerensky offensive. But it was also connected to the demands for autonomy in Ukraine, which caused a further dispute in the Russian Cabinet that led to the resignation of four ministers, all of whom were members of the Kadet Party. Like other non-Russian regions of the former empire, the Ukrainians had formed a new government, called the Central Rada, which had significant popular support. At the end of May 1917, the Central Rada sent a request to the Provisional Government that it recognize an autonomous Ukraine. The Russian side responded that such matters must wait until the convening of the Constituent Assembly. In turn, the Central Rada unilaterally proclaimed Ukraine to be an autonomous unit within Russia, causing profound disagreements among the Russian Cabinet.

By July, support for the Bolsheviks was increasing rapidly. They were the only party that seemed prepared to deal with urgent problems. In fact, Bolshevik strategy was encapsulated in three simple slogans: land to the peasants; bread to the workers; and down with the war. The party's total membership across Russia was around 240,000, encompassed by 162 party organizations. The largest single organization of Bolsheviks was the Petrograd Committee, which comprised about one-sixth of all members (40,000) and had more than doubled in the period April–July. The total membership in Moscow, however, was much lower, at only 15,000. Thus the flood to join the ranks of the Bolsheviks occurred most rapidly in Petrograd, and if the capital city was ready for a Bolshevik takeover in July 1917, the former capital, Moscow, certainly was not. Bolshevik membership was also very high in the Urals, and growing in the industrial regions of the Donbass, Kharkiv and Kyiv.

The July Days began with demonstrations by soldiers, many of whom were concerned that they would be asked to serve at the front; and by sailors from the Kronstadt naval base, who were frustrated with the lack of progress by the government in dealing with the most pressing questions. A Provisional Revolutionary Committee was established by the First Machine Gun Regiment on 16 July, and some 30,000 factory workers from the Putilov enterprise joined the assembled. As the crowd swelled once again in the streets of Petrograd, Bolshevik slogans were in evidence and there were demands that the Soviet should take power. The major question for the Bolsheviks was how to react to these mass demonstrations made in their name.

If the Bolshevik leadership did nothing, while their supporters had taken to the streets, then the question was how much longer would they be able to count on this support [5]. About 500,000 people were in the streets, or about a third of the entire population of the capital. Lenin had already declared in one public forum that the Bolsheviks were prepared to take power. Thus the Bolshevik leaders gave their reluctant assent to the uprising and decided to hold their own demonstration on 17 July under the slogan 'All power to the soviets!' They took this action even though they had no plans or strategy to take power. In retrospect it was probably the correct policy. It could serve as something of a dress rehearsal for the November uprising, as long as the government reaction was not too severe. In this way, the population would remain loyal to the party and its popularity would continue to increase. On the other hand, the lack of direction from Lenin may have caused the populace to have some doubts about Bolshevik commitment to the cause. At the end of the route of the demonstration was the Tauride Palace, which was soon surrounded by the marchers. Some Cabinet ministers were mocked and physically assaulted, including Viktor Chernov, the Minister of Agriculture [53]. Many of the protesters were Bolsheviks from the Petrograd Committee and its military organization.

Having reached this critical stage, a high-level Bolshevik meeting took place the same evening, chaired by Lenin, and decided that the demonstrations must be halted. Lenin was concerned about the timing of the event, believing that an uprising at this stage – the Bolsheviks were still a minority within the Soviet – was premature. If Lenin and the Central Committee had given their full backing to a revolt, then they would have succeeded only in giving power to the Mensheviks and Social Revolutionaries, who would have rejected it anyway. Some western historians regard the July Days as little more than a failed Bolshevik *putsch*. But this version of events seems misguided. The party responded to popular protests but without any plans for an armed uprising or a takeover of power.

While the uprising was in progress, rumours circulated that Lenin was a German agent (as the Germans had financed and organized his return to Russia), and this caused some regiments in Petrograd to reassert their loyalty to the government [65]. Because there was no conceivable purpose to the July Days once the Petrograd Soviet had refused to take power, the government, with the Soviet's backing, was able to restore order. The Bolshevik headquarters and the newspaper *Pravda* were raided on 18 July and the Trud printshop, which published the Bolshevik newspapers, was vandalized. On 19 July the government, supported by the Soviet leadership, declared martial law and a warrant was issued for the arrest of Lenin and other Bolshevik leaders. Anatoly Lunacharsky and Trotsky were arrested and imprisoned, along with several others. Lenin decided to flee, an action that has led some historians to accuse him of cowardice, though he did so reportedly on the instructions of his own Central Committee. Lenin evidently considered making a case against the government at a public trial, but he was afraid that there would be an attempt on his life were he to go to prison. In disguise he hid with friends and eventually fled to Finland, where once again he was separated temporarily from events in the capital. Prince Lvov resigned as Prime Minister and his place was taken by Kerensky on 21 July. On 6 August a new administration was formed: the Second Coalition government. It demanded a government of national salvation for the 'motherland and the revolution'. In addition, it vowed to continue with the war effort with the full backing of the western allies.

For the Bolsheviks, the immediate future looked bleak. Kerensky initiated a crackdown against all known revolutionaries within the army, and conducted a campaign to ascertain Bolsheviks among the factory workers. The period of conciliation of the March Revolution had ended. The Mensheviks and Social Revolutionaries were often torn between their sentiments and their beliefs. While their sympathies were often with the demonstrators, they believed firmly that the priority was to preserve the fragile power that had been attained with such joy and euphoria in the spring. To do otherwise, they believed, would be irresponsible. Consequently, rather than the watchdog over the actions of the government, the SR and Menshevik leaders of the Soviet also became closely associated with it. After the July Days, the goals of both organs were so close that they fused temporarily. Under these circumstances, Lenin's proud slogan of 'All power to the soviets!' appeared farcical and was dropped after the uprising was suppressed. For the moment there could be no possibility of gaining power through the soviets.

Kerensky's position seemed stronger after the failure of the July Days. Early in August he moved his office and that of the Cabinet to the Winter Palace. All parties continued to call for the convocation of the Constituent Assembly, and as a prelude to its election, on 25 August, Kerensky called together a gathering by the name of the Moscow State Conference, a transparent attempt to win backing for his government among the elite of Russian society. The English historian, E.H. Carr referred to the conference as 'a wordy fiasco' [51]. Held in the Bolshoy Theatre, it included army officers, former members of all the previous Dumas since 1907, members of the propertied classes, cooperatives, the clergy, teachers and lawyers. Greetings were sent to conference delegates by US president, Woodrow Wilson. The Bolsheviks attempted to incite the workers of Moscow to a general strike during the conference and did not participate in the discussions. Addressing the conference, Kerensky reiterated his commitment to the war effort, while declaring the need to restore order and stability in the armed forces and the country. The Moscow State Conference was less a demonstration of support for Kerensky than a symbol of a power struggle between the Prime Minister and the man he had appointed Commander-in-Chief of the Russian armed forces on 31 July, General Lavr Kornilov.

THE KORNILOV REVOLT AND AFTERMATH

Many conservatives regarded Kerensky's response to the July Days and to the Bolshevik insurgents as weak and half-hearted. Kornilov, a dour general with most of his experience in the Far East, seemed a better alternative. Moreover, he believed that Kerensky had endowed him with significant powers with a dubious comment that he should keep his troops on the alert to repulse any form of trouble. Kornilov did much more than this. From the moment he took office, he began to weed out of the army unreliable elements and even entire regiments. He established in turn 33 shock battalions and added to them reliable Cossack units. In so doing he received support from some disaffected former Cabinet ministers, such as Mikhail Rodzianko and Pavel Milyukov. The former even sent a gushing telegram to the general, adding to the latter's already inflated sense of his own importance with the comments 'In this frightening hour of bitter trial, the intelligentsia of Russia look to you with hope and trust' [61].

On 3 September the port of Riga fell to the advancing Germans, a cataclysmic event because it appeared to leave the road to Petrograd open. Soviet propaganda implies that Kornilov deliberately pulled back troops from the area in order to allow the Germans to advance and subsequently take the capital. But there is little evidence to support such a claim. Kornilov was loyal to the allies rather than the Germans [*Doc. 6*]. The fall of Riga, however, was probably the catalyst that prompted Kornilov to march his troops on Petrograd. Just the day before, he had ordered the Cossacks and a Wild Division of troops from the Caucasus to advance to within striking distance of both Moscow and Petrograd. Kornilov left no doubt of his intentions. His goal was to enter the capital and round up and hang the leading Bolsheviks, including Lenin (how he intended to capture Lenin is unclear). Kornilov seemed to have significant support, including financiers, former Duma and Provisional Government Cabinet members, and the western allies. The result of a Kornilov victory would have been a military dictatorship in Russia.

There followed a bizarre exchange of messages between Kornilov and Kerensky that has long baffled historians, some of whom have claimed that the Prime Minister must have been involved to some extent in the plot. Kerensky soon discovered that Russian troops led by his Commander-in-Chief were marching on Petrograd and demanded an explanation. He was informed by his emissary that the troops intended to restore order, whereupon Kerensky countermanded the order and demanded that the march be stopped. When Kornilov refused, then his treachery was evident. The capital was in a state of panic, but virtually all political elements were willing to support the government against Kornilov – the possible exception was the Kadet Party, all of whose members resigned from the Cabinet at this time. On 9 September Kerensky dismissed his Commander-in-Chief, though the order was simply ignored by the general. He was also provided with emergency powers to take action by his Cabinet.

Kerensky's problem was that he lacked popular support among the workers, soldiers and sailors. Consequently, he declared a general amnesty, releasing Bolsheviks from prison and allowing the members of the factory Red Guards to arm themselves. Over 13,000 Red Guard troops were assembled in Petrograd, with particularly large groups in areas such as the Vyborg district. A Committee for the Struggle of the People against the Counter-Revolution was established, a coalition body that was supported by all the socialist parties. Petrograd was a hive of feverish activity in preparation for Kornilov's attack. About 3,000 sailors arrived from Kronstadt to defend the capital. The insurgence, however, ended in anti-climax. Kornilov's troops fraternized with workers and railway men *en route*. The much-feared Wild Division was greeted by a Muslim delegation sent from Petrograd and refused to advance. Kornilov was arrested and the commander of his leading column of troops committed suicide.

The actions taken against Kornilov united the capital as never before. More important, however, they altered fundamentally the balance of power. The factory workers of the Red Guard retained their weapons, and the feeling in the capital was that the decisive action against the revolt had been taken by troops loyal to the Bolsheviks. The collapse of the Kornilov revolt then was less a triumph for the government than one for the Bolsheviks. Having released the Bolsheviks and permitted them to take action, Kerensky relinquished much of his authority in the city. The government tried to regroup by forming a new coalition with the Soviet. Russia was declared a republic on 14 September, and the Mensheviks and Social Revolutionaries, who still retained a majority in the Petrograd Soviet (it would dissipate with a new election later in the month), gave the government their full support. The Bolsheviks, who were the fastest growing element in political life and now with enhanced prestige, had become the main opposition. The power of the government was beginning to crumble.

THE GROWING CRISIS

In the summer and autumn of 1917 Russia was facing a desperate economic situation brought on largely by continued participation in the First World War. The war was a major drain on the economy and main facets of the latter were in a state of near collapse on the eve of the Bolshevik seizure of power [*Doc. 7*]. The first problem was that the communications system –

and especially the railroads – had become overloaded. Raw materials were not reaching the factories, which in turn shut down and frequently locked out their workers. The production of essential resources, such as coal, iron and steel, fell dramatically as the war continued, but never more so than in 1917 when output dropped by as much as 60 per cent. The steel mills and coal mines of Ukraine's Donbass were virtually at a standstill and unemployment rose accordingly.

The problem of financing the war was particularly acute. The government ran up huge debts, about a quarter of which were owed to its allies. The total state debt was estimated at 50 trillion rubles in 1917. To pay for the war, the Provisional Government printed more money in paper bills that were called 'Kerenky' by the public. Hyperinflation had occurred by the summer and food prices rose astronomically. Though the workers received wage increases, these fell well behind the rises in prices, and as noted, increasing numbers of workers were locked out of their factories or unemployed. In August 1917 the government doubled the price of bread without offering a compensatory wage rise. For months there had been long queues outside bread shops. By September and October, the urban population was increasingly destitute, while in the countryside the loss of the male population meant that large areas went unharvested. Peasant insurgencies were frequent even in the late tsarist period, but in 1917 they were widespread and constant. The police reported over 3,000 'violations' of the land law in September alone. The peasants coveted the land of the great estates and in many areas local soviets had already taken matters into their own hands.

There were no obvious solutions open to the government. The nation was clearly war-weary and the army in no shape to continue the fight. The Kerensky government had few ideas and little public support. The only question was how much longer it could last and with what it might be replaced. At the sixth Congress of the Bolshevik Party (officially designated as the RSDWP [b]), held on 8–16 August, Lenin sent directions from his hiding place in Finland that success could be gained not merely by a workers' uprising, but rather from an alliance of the urban proletariat and the poorest stratum of the peasantry (in Russian, the *bednyak* stratum). Lenin's party had barely a foothold in the countryside but the party platform was adopted to meet the demands that emanated from the rural regions. Though the peasants generally remained loyal to the Social Revolutionary Party (insofar as they retained party loyalties), they could have few objections to Bolshevik policies as long as they coincided with events taking place at the village level. This was another example of Lenin's flexibility in the quest for power.

The route to state authority, however, still lay through the Soviets and within them the balance of power was changing. The Mensheviks and Social Revolutionaries were compromised by their association with an unpopular government. By 13 September, the Bolshevik delegates for the first time were in a majority in the Petrograd Soviet. At once they began to put forward motions to test the strength of their vote, and on 18 September Trotsky pushed through a vote of non-confidence in the Soviet leadership under Chkeidze, which succeeded by 519 votes to 414, with 67 abstentions, with the decisive votes coming from soldiers. Chkeidze was obliged to resign, and on 8 October he was replaced as Chairman by Trotsky. On 18 September, the Bolsheviks also gained a majority in the Moscow Soviet. In the city elections that took place in the following month in Moscow, the SR and Menshevik vote collapsed; that of the Kadets remained stable, while the Bolshevik vote rose by over 250 per cent. Political life was becoming polarized. By this time, acting on the instructions of Lenin, who was inexplicably still in hiding in Finland sending frantic orders to his party, the slogan 'All power to the soviets!' was revived. For the first time it had begun to make sense.

The Kerensky government decided to hold yet another assembly, this time in Petrograd, and entitled the Democratic Conference, in order to try to unite the moderate groups. The representation of the soviets at this conference was such that their members could not command a majority. However, the conference revealed only the further divisions within the groups that had held power over the turbulent summer of 1917, a time as complex and changing as 1991. Chkeidze and Tsereteli put forward a motion at the conference to form a new coalition government, but it was defeated. Instead, a Pre-Parliament was formed called the All-Russian Democratic Council, which would be a prelude to elections to the long-awaited Constituent Assembly. The Pre-Parliament worried Lenin, who felt that it might encourage a more conciliatory move among the Bolsheviks. Kamenev, who appears to have spent various moments of late 1917 opposing the views of his leader at critical junctures, advocated that the Bolsheviks join the Pre-Parliament and form a Left Opposition. Instead, the Bolsheviks attended the Pre-Parliament only long enough to read out a derisive declaration and then walked out. The image one unavoidably gets is of government leaders debating endlessly while all around them their house was burning down. On 8 October, the same day on which Trotsky became Chairman of the Petrograd Soviet, Kerensky founded a Third Coalition government, which contained representation from the Kadets once again.

The polarization of political life also caused deep divisions within the SRs and the Mensheviks. The former split into two during the Democratic Conference, when a breakaway Leftist group was formed under Boris Kamkov and Mariya Spiridonova, which supported the policy of all land to the peasants, bringing their platform close to that of the Bolsheviks. The mainstream party, much larger in size, remained firmly in the Cabinet. The Mensheviks also had begun to divide into two factions: the so-called Defensists who were on the right of the party and the Menshevik Internationalists under Lenin's former friend Martov. As Orlando Figes has noted, the city meeting of the Menshevik Party in Petrograd in September had to be cancelled because it was inquorate. The Mensheviks and their SR partners had made too many compromises of their principles, particularly their support for Russia's continued commitment to the war. In trying to save the revolution and stabilize the Russian government, they engineered their own demise. What was occurring in Russia was essentially a vacuum of power.

CHAPTER THREE

THE NOVEMBER REVOLUTION

THE UPRISING

Lenin was in a state of almost feverish anxiety by October 1917, constantly sending messages to the Bolshevik Central Committee about the need to take action. The party was not dragging its feet, but there were serious doubts about the necessity of an armed uprising at that time. On 7 October a conference was held by the Central Committee of the party and the Petrograd Committee that embraced the notion of a takeover of power. A few days later, a meeting of the Moscow organization resolved that advantage must be taken of the mass support for the party that was so evident on the streets. In this period – the precise date is uncertain – Lenin returned to the capital still in disguise and stayed at the home of a family friend, M.V. Fofanova. Sources agree that it was on Lenin's initiative that a Central Committee meeting on 23 October discussed and passed a motion that supported an immediate insurrection [*Doc. 8*]. The motion was passed by 10 votes to 2, with Kamenev and Zinoviev the dissenters. Several Bolsheviks were absent, some of whom would probably have voted against the motion. After the vote a Political Bureau was elected, composed of seven members (including Lenin, Trotsky and Stalin). The Political Bureau, however, was not the main instrument of the uprising. In all likelihood it never even held a formal meeting.

Kamenev and Zinoviev were so concerned about plans to take power that they circulated a letter to all Bolshevik organizations protesting against the idea and even published their objections on the pages of *Novaya Zhizn'* (New Life, a non-party newspaper), in the process informing the government authorities of what was afoot. Lenin was furious and declared in a letter to fellow party members that he would demand their removal from the party (a comment evidently issued in the heat of the moment since he never carried this through). It is unlikely, however, that the government was ignorant of such plans. A second resolution was passed by a meeting of an expanded Bolshevik Central Committee on 29 October. Kamenev and Zinoviev once again opposed it, but were outvoted by 20 votes to 2. However, the vote does not necessarily indicate approval of the precise timing of an uprising, but rather consent in principle. Trotsky and others were concerned that the uprising be timed to coincide with the Second All-Russian Congress of Soviets, at which, it was anticipated, the Bolsheviks would have a majority and be able to announce that the soviets had taken power. Lenin continued to insist that the armed uprising must precede the Congress. On 12 October he wrote an article to this effect, entitled 'The crisis has ripened'. However, the decisive action, rather than rhetoric, was taken by his fellow Bolsheviks.

On 28 October, in response to a motion by a Menshevik deputy, the Petrograd Soviet formed a Military Revolutionary Committee (MRC). This was an organ similar to the Bolsheviks' own military organization that had achieved some success in winning the support of the Petrograd garrison and sailors of the Baltic Fleet and Kronstadt in the July uprising. When the MRC held its first meeting on 2 November, it elected a bureau of five members (three Bolsheviks and two Social Revolutionaries), while the overall membership was 66 (including 48 Bolsheviks and 14 Left SRs). The initial leader of the MRC was a Left SR, P. Lazimir, and subsequently a Bolshevik, N.I. Podvoisky. Since the MRC was subordinated to the Petrograd Soviet, however, its real director was the Chairman of the Soviet, Trotsky. The MRC was to prove the crucial organ in winning the support or neutrality of the military garrison and fleet, and in ensuring the readiness and preparation of the Red Guards, whose numbers had swelled to 23,000 in Petrograd by this date. The MRC communicated directly with a 'military revolutionary centre' composed of five Bolsheviks: Sverdlov, Stalin, Bubnov, Uritsky and Dzerzhinsky.

Soviet sources stress the extensive preparations for the uprising and the widespread support for the Bolsheviks in the major cities. They neglect to mention, however, that the crucial role in these final days was played by Trotsky. This was his finest hour. His speech at the Fortress of St Peter and Paul was a key factor in winning over the troops to the Bolshevik cause. It was Trotsky's role as Chairman of the Soviet that was the decisive factor, rather than his work in the Bolshevik Central Committee. This fortress was the basic source of defence for the Winter Palace. Had the troops chosen to defend the seat of government then the revolution could have been bloody indeed. Lenin by contrast was drafting letters to the last, cajoling his followers to take action [*Doc. 8*]. His last such letter to the Central Committee was sent on 6 November, in which he declared that if the Bolsheviks hesitated, then all would be lost. As the Second Congress was scheduled to open on 7 November, however, and the uprising had to be successful prior to that event – at least in theory – it can be safely surmised that Lenin's final letters were superfluous, and reflected only the mood of a man in an acute state of nervous tension and anxiety. This was Lenin's revolution, but on the day itself he was a secondary actor.

It is estimated that if one simply adds all the armed forces that were now in the Bolshevik camp, supporters or sympathizers, the total was around 300,000 soldiers, sailors, and Red Guards [57]. What sort of forces could Kerensky's government muster? The answer is about one-tenth of that of the revolutionaries. Kerensky therefore made one last effort to reverse the situation with a preemptive strike at the Bolsheviks and the MRC. On the morning of 5 November, a decision was announced to begin criminal proceedings against the MRC, and to round up the Bolshevik leaders after the arrival of more reliable troops from outside the capital. Early in the morning of 6 November, the Bolshevik printing presses were halted, and two newspapers, *Rabochii Put'* and *Soldatskaya pravda*, were shut down and extant copies confiscated. The *Avrora* cruiser, which was anchored opposite the Winter Palace, and known to contain a Bolshevik crew, was ordered out to sea.

Much has been made of this government counter-strike. It has even been suggested that it forced the Bolsheviks to act when they did. This viewpoint has little credibility. Bolshevik preparations for the uprising were in place. Based at the Smolny Institute, the Bolshevik headquarters that had formerly been a high school for girls, the Bolsheviks had preparations well in hand for the uprising. The counter-strike was Kerensky's final, rather feeble attempt to halt it. Kerensky himself, with his dramatic imagination, may not have realized the weakness of his position. He reminds one of an actor who believed that whenever he returned to the stage he could command the attention of an audience. But within a few hours, the MRC had countermanded his order to the *Avrora* and the cruiser returned. The Trud printing presses were at work again by the late morning of 6 November. Lenin, still in disguise, made his way to the Smolny Institute close to midnight on this same day where he would wait for news that the insurrection had been successful. Within two hours he received reports that the railway stations, central telegraph office, post office, power stations and main telephone exchange were all in Bolshevik hands [53; 68].

By 10 a.m., the MRC was able to issue, perhaps prematurely, Lenin's resolution 'To the citizens of Russia'. The Provisional Government, it declared, had been overthrown and state power had passed into the hands of the Military Revolutionary Committee of the Petrograd Soviet. This proclamation was swiftly telegraphed across Russia so that it would be widely known before the start of the Congress. Three hours later, the Marinsky Palace was captured and the Pre-Parliament disbanded. The Winter Palace, however, had not yet been taken. It was defended only by some 3,000 troops, including military cadets, Cossack units, members of the Women's Battalion and what few supporters of the government could be mustered. But the reason it took so long to fall into the hands of the Bolsheviks was that the Kronstadt sailors, who had been given the job of arresting the government ministers, had failed to turn up. The two events that were later to symbolize the revolution in Soviet films – the firing of shots from the *Avrora* and the 'storming of the Winter Palace' – were largely mythical. The timing of events suggests that the Winter Palace hardly needed to be stormed. Only 15 minutes after the cruiser fired two blanks, the cadets and Cossack units had laid down their arms, and shortly thereafter the Women's Battalion raised a white flag. When Antonov-Ovseenko arrived on the scene, followed by Red Guards to make the arrest of the ministers, they all entered through the main gate without encountering any resistance [53; 100].

The Winter Palace was occupied by large groups of Red Guards and sailors in the early hours of 8 November. Kerensky was not there. He had fled the capital on the previous morning in a car loaned to him by the US Embassy. His intention was to travel to the Northern Front and return with an army. The ministers of the Cabinet, however, had remained in session and were all rounded up and arrested. What had occurred therefore was largely a bloodless uprising and takeover of power. There was some resistance initially from the Women's Battalion, but the latter had only been appointed to shame their menfolk into fighting for the defence of the government. In terms of casualties, the figures were very low – almost certainly less than ten. In fact, many people in the capital were unaware of what was happening. There was no general strike as in the March events; public transport continued to run, cinemas and theatres were open. The events of both March and July appeared more dramatic. The acquisition of power was to be far easier than its preservation afterward.

At 2.30 p.m. on 7 November, the Petrograd Soviet held an emergency session chaired by Trotsky at the Smolny Institute. Lenin made his first public appearance of the day and received a standing ovation. Trotsky related the events of the day in order to prepare the Bolsheviks for the Congress of Soviets, which began later in the evening. Lenin did not attend the first session of the Congress, though the Bolsheviks, supported by the Left SRs, clearly had a majority of the delegates. Of 660 delegates, the Bolsheviks had 390. A presidium was elected composed of 22 people, of whom 14 were Bolsheviks, including Lenin and Trotsky, and even Kamenev and Zinoviev, who had soon been restored to favour. The Mensheviks and mainstream SRs made their displeasure at the uprising evident by walking out of the Congress, together with a group from the Jewish Bund [*Doc. 9*]. Trotsky uncharitably consigned them to the 'garbage heap of history'. The Bolsheviks saw no problems in sharing power with the Left SRs, but initially that party felt that the ruling coalition should be much broader. The Congress began its session after 10.30 p.m., and by 3 a.m. the following morning it received the news that the Winter Palace had fallen and the Cabinet members (excepting Kerensky) detained. An hour later, Lunacharsky, for the Bolsheviks, read Lenin's manifesto announcing that the Congress had assumed political authority. It was accepted almost unanimously.

The final act of this tumultous period was the appearance of Lenin at the second session of the Congress on the evening of 8 November, his first extended public appearance in the capital. At his behest, the Congress issued two decrees: the Decree on Peace [*Doc. 10*] and the Decree on Land [*Doc. 11*]. Subsequently a new government was formed with a suitably revolutionary name: the Council of People's Commissars. Lenin was the chairman, Trotsky was given control of foreign affairs, Stalin of nationalities, and three MRC leaders – Pavel Dybenko, Nikolay Krylenko, and Antonov-Ovseenko – shared military affairs [*Doc. 12*]. All the leaders of the government were Bolsheviks. The revolution had triumphed in Petrograd.

Elsewhere the Bolsheviks faced a more difficult task, particularly because the lines between the Bolsheviks and the other socialist parties were never so clearly drawn. In Moscow, those loyal to the Provisional Government, encompassed in a Committee of Public Safety, seized control over the Kremlin and mounted a staunch defence against the Military Revolutionary Committee of the Moscow Soviet. After a bloody conflict lasting for one week and resulting in over 1,000 casualties, the Soviet authorities were able to take over the city of Moscow. In other centres, the fighting sometimes lasted for months. Kyiv, for example, was occupied by the Bolsheviks only in February 1918 and then only for a short period [103]. In central Russia, the Bolsheviks took control in the spring and early summer of 1918. In other areas, there was little communication with the distant capital and former capital and locals took things into their own hands. In some places soviets dominated by Mensheviks and SRs took power. In Kronstadt, the sailors proclaimed a soviet republic [109].

THE CONSTITUENT ASSEMBLY

Having taken power, the Bolsheviks were to some extent restricted by their promises to the population. They had been very strident in their demands for the convocation of the Constituent Assembly, the elections to which had been fixed prior to the uprising for 25 November 1917. The Bolsheviks had little time to use their new authority to influence the outcome of these elections, which were a test case of the popularity of the various political parties on a nationwide basis. The results were embarrassing for Lenin's party. The Social Revolutionary Party – undivided on the ballots – received 58 per cent of all votes, compared to 25 per cent for the Bolsheviks, 13 per cent for the Kadets and their allies on the political right, and a feeble 4 per cent for the Mensheviks. Translated into seats, this gave the SRs 410 out of 707 filled seats (the Constituent Assembly had been created as an 800-seat body, but about 90 seats were never contested), whereas the Bolsheviks had

175, the Kadets 17 and the Mensheviks 16. A powerful element in the assembly was the non-Russian groups, which had between them over 80 seats and were strongly opposed to the Bolsheviks [51].

Thus less than three weeks after the revolution, the Bolsheviks had seemingly been rejected by the population. Would they accept the democratic mandate and renounce power? There were several possible options. The first was to delay the convocation of the new assembly, thereby giving the Bolsheviks time to take measures against their major opposition. Lenin began by forming an alliance with the Left SRs, who were permitted three seats in the new Cabinet: agriculture, justice, and posts and telegraphs. In this way the Bolsheviks could be said to be sharing power with another socialist party. Moreover – and Lenin was quick to take up this point – it could be claimed that the elections were no longer valid since the SR party in its original form no longer existed. On 26 December Lenin published his *Theses on the Constituent Assembly*, a pamphlet that attempted to belittle the importance of the Constituent Assembly [12]. Lenin argued that under a bourgeois regime it had made sense for his party to support calls for the assembly, but after the revolution a higher democratic body had emerged, namely the Soviet.

Lenin's resort to linguistic subterfuge could not camouflage the real situation, however, which was that the Bolsheviks, though popular in the large urban centres, among the soldiers of the North and Western Fronts, and among the sailors of the Baltic Fleet, did not have mass support in the countryside. Zemstvo councils, dominated by the mainstream SRs, still wielded great influence in the villages. Little could be done about such support in the short term. Instead, Lenin decided to concentrate on the target of the Kadet Party. Prior to the convocation of the Constituent Assembly, the Kadets were outlawed and their leaders arrested. The official pretext was the formation of a group in Petrograd called the All-Russian League for the Defence of the Constituent Assembly, allegedly led by the Kadets and supported by the Entente powers, as represented by the British ambassador, George Buchanan, who had unwisely let it be known that the British government was prepared to accept the Constituent Assembly as the legitimate government of Russia. Subsequently sailors and Red Guards rounded up the Kadet leaders on 11 December.

Even some western historians have accepted the Bolshevik version of events describing a Kadet uprising [51]. The uprising, however, was a Bolshevik creation. The Kadets were no longer in a position to have a decisive influence over events. Rather the Bolsheviks had begun to act in a peremptory and undemocratic fashion, and their new allies the Left SRs were quick to decry the arbitrary arrests. Even some of the Bolshevik delegates to the assembly were dismayed (they were quickly replaced). Such actions had been unfamiliar during the period of opposition. Once in power, however, and confronted with its minority status, the Bolshevik Party leadership began to use force and repression to remove its enemies. The road to the Civil War thus began directly after the takeover of power, catalysed by the Constituent Assembly, the first roadblock encountered by the new government. The Bolsheviks decided to let the assembly meet, in the Tauride Palace, on 18 January 1918. They failed to have their own spokesperson, Yakob Sverdlov, elected Chairman of the assembly, but with the threat of coercion – manifested by Kronstadt sailors in the galleries playfully pointing their guns at the heads of the new deputies – he soon took the floor regardless.

Sverdlov, a ruthless administrator with a style not dissimilar to that of Stalin, tried to cajole those gathered into accepting the Declaration of the Rights of Working and Exploited Peoples already passed by Lenin's new government. The SR majority had little time for such manipulation and refused, whereupon the Bolshevik deputies walked out of the assembly. Reportedly the atmosphere in the streets outside the Tauride Palace was tense. Thousands of demonstrators had carried placards bearing the slogan 'All power to the Constituent Assembly!' and their opponents, comprised mainly of sailors, carried placards declaring 'All power to the soviets!' For the Bolsheviks, the Constituent Assembly had become a rallying point for all those opposed to their revolution, or, in their view, the enemies of the working people of Russia. After the departure of the Bolsheviks, the Left SRs soon walked out as well, leaving the remaining delegates to indulge in prolonged debate until the early hours of the morning. Tired guards finally prevailed on the deputies to go home. They were not permitted to reconvene. On 20 January the Soviet Executive Committee issued a decree formally dissolving the assembly.

The Constituent Assembly took place in Petrograd, the seat of the revolution. For many deputies from the rural regions, taking their seats was a frightening affair. The capital was a virtual armed camp of Bolshevik sailors and Red Guards. The Bolsheviks had tried to manipulate the assembly, but having failed in the attempt they decided to dissolve it instead. It represented a rival body of power and was to become a symbol for those who opposed the Bolsheviks during the civil war. The question has been raised as to why the majority of delegates, having come so far, simply went home without protest. One reason was the novelty of the democratic process in Russia. A second was the naivety of some of the delegates who were unfamiliar with politics in the capital. But the third is that the delegates were in no position to mount a protest against the display of armed force offered by Lenin's party. Almost immediately following the dissolution of the assembly, on 21 January, there was convened the Third All-Russian Congress of Soviets of Workers' and Soldiers' Deputies, closely followed by the Third All-Russian Congress of Peasants' Deputies.

The inference was clear: the Bolsheviks were presenting the assembly as the higher form of authority, a point strengthened when, at the behest of Sverdlov, the two Congresses decided to merge on 26 January. The representation at the peasant congress was dubious: over 85 per cent of all delegates professed adherence to either the Bolsheviks or the Left SRs. The Congress was more symbolic than creative. It took the step that the Constituent Assembly had declined to do, by formally proclaiming the Declaration of the Rights of the Working and Exploited Peoples, a grandiloquent document that announced the abolition of private property, the end of all exploitation, the nationalization of banks, the creation of a new army, and the founding of a Supreme Economic Council, which presaged the new policy of War Communism that was to emerge later in the year. Along with the Declaration, the Congress also declared the creation of a Russian Soviet Federated Socialist Republic (abbreviated as Soviet Russia).

REVOLUTION OR *COUP D'ETAT?*

Since the dissolution of the Soviet Union, there has been renewed focus on the armed uprising that brought the Bolsheviks to power on 7 November 1917. A process of de-Leninization has occurred in Russia, which has bolstered the views of those western historians who denied the significance of that date as a great victorious revolution. Most western accounts, while they disagree on many fundamentals, tend to concur that the events of 7 November constituted a *coup d'état* by a minority party and that these events brought great misfortune to the people of Russia. The opening of the Russian archives has brought new revelations that demonstrate the ruthlessness of the Bolsheviks, and Lenin in particular [14]. A protracted discussion on the similarities of Leninism and Stalinism now seems to some extent redundant. Clearly Lenin as a leader was much more cruel than many western historians had hitherto surmised. These debates, however, do not necessarily signify that the events of 7 November can be dismissed as a virtual *putsch* by gangsters, who were then obliged to hang on to power by brute force.

The historian might instead make a distinction between the actions of the Bolshevik leaders prior to and after the takeover of power. In the period April–October 1917, all Lenin's speeches and actions indicate that the question of taking power was paramount in his mind. His single-mindedness attracted the previously aloof Trotsky to his side and it often horrified and antagonized his longtime associates, such as Zinoviev and Kamenev. Even the future dictator Stalin did not initially comprehend the need to keep a distance from the other socialist parties in the euphoric conditions of the spring of 1917 [37]. Having said this, however, it also has to be noted that Lenin did not create the conditions for Bolshevik rule; he merely took advantage of them, coming to power at a time when no other party was willing to take such a radical step. That he was able to do so was a result of a vacuum of power at the centre in Petrograd. There was no longer any support for the Provisional Government, whose leaders would surely have been swept away in any vote for a Constituent Assembly. All the crucial decisions had been delayed pending the convocation of this body, thus there was little reason for the government to prolong its existence.

The above argument hardly renders Lenin a democrat, but it does take into account that there was a growing groundswell of support for the Bolsheviks in the capital at the time of the 7 November uprising. By that time they were the most popular party, whether or not that support was equivocal or based on a 'least of all evils' deduction on the part of the electorate. Yet where those who might sympathize with the choice faced by Lenin run into a stumbling block is the need for the armed uprising, the unsavoury if relatively bloodless actions that saw the Bolsheviks take power on the backs of the Red Guards, sailors and soldiers in the streets of the capital. Could they not have waited for the Second Congress of Soviets, in the knowledge that they already had a commanding majority in the Petrograd Soviet? Was there a need for the Military Revolutionary Committee?

The Bolsheviks, however, had tried (albeit half-heartedly) and failed once to take power in July. They could not afford the possibility of a second failure. As far as Lenin was concerned, there was a moment at which the party could come to power. Once that moment was past, it may not – indeed probably would not – recur. The other parties, the Mensheviks and the Social Revolutionaries, were either too confined to dogmatic Marxism or else too closely linked to the Provisional Government to engineer a successful takeover. The Bolsheviks could have shared power with their fellow socialists, but in Lenin's view they were likely to become bogged down in endless debates. But why did the Provisional Government fail so abjectly? What happened to the utopian democratic experiment of 1917, a period that continued for years to bring wistful comments from the western democracies, bolstered by somewhat one-sided memoirs from its former leaders such as Kerensky?

First, it was always a temporary government, without a popular mandate. It co-existed with the Petrograd Soviet as long as the latter organization allowed it to do so. On several occasions – Order No. 1 is the best example – it proved powerless to take action against a rising revolutionary sentiment. Second, it failed to deal with the three basic problems of the day, which were, in order of importance: the continuation of the war; food for the population; and the land question in the countryside (which is placed last since that matter to some extent was being resolved locally without the intrusion of the authorities). Only the Bolsheviks focused exclusively on these three questions, no matter how cynical their motives may have been. By November, the other socialist parties were all closely associated with the government. Their leaders were part of the Cabinet, and in the minds of the population they would forever be associated with the decision to continue the war, to mount a new offensive, to arrest the Red Guards during the July Days, to round up the Bolshevik leaders at the same time, to restore the death penalty at the front, and other decisions that were highly unpopular.

Thus while Lenin's party could not necessarily hold power, it was not a difficult or unpopular decision for them to take it when the possibility arose. The revolution of 7 November may have had its farcical side and its leader may not have been noted for his bravery, as Pipes notes [68]. It may have seen little bloodshed and perhaps most citizens of Petrograd remained unsure for some time what had actually occurred. Yet it was a revolution, undertaken by force, by a party that had widespread support in the capital. It resulted in a change of government. The argument that the Bolshevik revolution was a popular uprising seems plausible, no matter how undemocratic the Bolsheviks proved to be after the event [93; 100].

THE PIPES DEBATE

In western historiography on the Russian Revolution, a turning point of sorts was reached in 1990 with the publication of Richard Pipes's *The Russian Revolution*, a magisterial, imperious study that refocused the debate on Lenin and the Bolshevik Party [68]. Subsequently, Pipes has provided further volumes, but they have not had the same dramatic impact of the 1990 book. The latter received a mixed and raucous reception from the western academic community. The timing was remarkable. A book long in preparation was published on the eve of the dissolution of the Soviet Union, a time when disillusionment with the Soviet system was at its peak. Pipes's book was thus assured of a warm reception in Russia because of its anti-Lenin stance and highly critical account of how the Bolsheviks came to power, their cruelty and viciousness, and the personal failings of the once-revered leader, V.I. Lenin. Pipes had compiled all these failings assiduously, while setting aside and effectively shelving any virtues the Bolshevik leader may have had. This sweeping indictment of Lenin and Bolshevism eventually received several responses from western scholars. On a number of grounds, the criticism of Pipes has been severe.

The debate is put into perspective by the American scholar Ronald Grigor Suny, who notes that for five decades after the November Revolution an 'orthodox' interpretation pervaded in the West, which maintained that an 'illegal' government had been established in Petrograd that used violence and terror to preserve itself. This interpretation focused on the political aspects of the Bolshevik takeover and largely ignored social issues and a growing rift between top and bottom in Russian society. It argued that the weak government founded after the fall of tsarism collapsed as a result of conspiracy by the Bolsheviks, a party that did not represent its followers and had no real foundation among the populace. If this interpretation was correct, then all the evils associated with the Soviet regime (the purges, the Famine in Ukraine, and others) originated not with Stalin, but with the party that seized power in November from a government fatally weakened by the effects of the First World War [119].

In the 1970s and 1980s, this interpretation came under scrutiny from social and labour historians who sought to explain some of the inconsistencies therein and to assess the impact of workers, soldiers and peasants on the course of events in 1917. These historians also questioned the hitherto accepted monolithic nature of the Bolshevik Party and its desire for power at various junctures in this pivotal year. Their works broadened knowledge of the revolution by providing a better understanding of the changing circumstances and goals during critical periods. They indicated, for example, that Lenin in particular was not anxious to seize power in the spring of 1917 and that there were deep rifts within the party [25; 62; 76; 79; 87; 89; 90]. Suny points out that the social interpretations have been associated by their critics with left-wing politics and Marxist ideology, citing Walter Laqueur's dismissive comment that ultimately the revolution was the work of one man (Lenin) [119]. Nevertheless, these works (which clearly were not all written by Marxists, leftists, or even their sympathizers) fundamentally changed the traditional perspective of the November Revolution. An interpretation that coincided with Cold War politics had been undermined by studies that took into account a wider perspective and indicated that the Bolsheviks were considerably closer in their views to the aspirations of the workers and soldiers than had previously been thought.

Pipes's book reasserted the traditional view in a unique way. Rather than debate the various viewpoints advanced by social historians, he simply ignores them. There is no indication in his *Russian Revolution* that such works even exist. The first part of the book continues a theme developed in an earlier work (*Russia Under the Old Regime*), namely that the tsarist government was a patrimonial system which evoked little patriotism or loyalty but was nonetheless constructed over several centuries and perhaps appropriate for Russian conditions. Part 2, however, transforms the thesis into a polemic. Pipes demonstrates both contempt and intense hatred for intellectuals (i.e. the Bolsheviks and their leader, Lenin). According to one critic, Pipes's book depicts everyone as a villain with the notable exceptions of Nikolay II and Lavr Kornilov, and the chief villain is Lenin, who is portrayed as rigid, unchanging, single-minded, not to mention cowardly and contemptible at every turn [118].

Perhaps the most controversial part of Pipes's book is his view that the Bolsheviks staged three attempted *putsches* in 1917, in April, June and July, disregarding eyewitness accounts and Lenin's personal intervention to restrain the masses. According to Peter Kenez [118], the only evidence cited for Bolshevik involvement in the events of April and June is that a minor Bolshevik persuaded supporters to carry banners bearing slogans such as 'All power to the Soviets!' Similarly, the depiction of Lenin as a coward derives from a single account, that of the wife of the leader of the Bolshevik faction in the Second Duma, who was writing in 1923 [117]. Pipes compares the July Uprising to Hitler's abortive *putsch* in a Munich beer hall in 1923, an unfortunate comparison that is compounded by later astonishing comments that the Bolshevik regime was the precursor of Stalinism and German 'Nazism', and that Lenin's hatred for the bourgeoisie was analogous to Hitler's hatred for the Jews [68; 119].

The work of Richard Pipes cannot be dismissed as sheer propaganda. He remains one of the world's leading historians on the Russian Revolution and parts of his book are insightful and helpful to readers. However, the work is marred by its bitterness and anger. Moreover, it is selective in its treatment, so that facts that might construe different interpretations of events are simply omitted. Above all, the decision of the author to ignore numerous works, ostensibly on the grounds that these sorts of interpretation lack merit or credibility, is unacceptable. It is blinkered history reminiscent in its one-sidedness of the versions of the revolution produced in the Soviet period. Above all, it assumes the primacy – if not infallibility – of political history over social interpretations. It ignores almost overwhelming social and economic forces with the argument that one man and his intellectual followers could control the passage of events, manipulate them for their own ends, and ultimately construct a state that was malevolent and intolerant, a ruthless dictatorship. While few would argue that that dictatorship did emerge before long (as noted below the Bolshevik regime applied mass terror very shortly after the takeover of power), the forces in play in 1917 were much more complex. It is true that the Bolsheviks were and would always be a minority in Russia. In the major cities, however, they were increasingly acceptable.

Finally, the reader must question the assessment of Lenin himself. Lenin was a complex character, highly disciplined, but at the same time flexible. Though a political animal, he was known to develop several close friendships (unlike, for example, Hitler and Stalin, with whom he is implicitly compared in Pipes's book). Lenin's motivations at various times remain debatable, but it seems simplistic to perceive his entire career as one bent on seizing power – in the early part of the twentieth century, for example, he appears to have despaired that the revolution would occur in his lifetime. He was practical enough also to know when the time was right for the Bolshevik uprising, and most sources suggest that he restrained the masses in April and June, and joined in the demonstrations of July only with marked reluctance. Pipes has demonized Lenin and the Bolsheviks, attributing the worst of motives to all their actions while often minimizing those of their equally ruthless opponents. On the other hand, the publication of Pipes's book revitalized interest in the November Revolution and sparked widespread debate. In a field in which works on the topic number in the thousands rather than the hundreds, that in itself is an achievement.

THE TREATY OF BREST-LITOVSK

The Bolsheviks had come to power with the promise of ending Russia's participation in the First World War. There was little chance, however, that the Entente powers would agree to such a proposal and they did not even bother to reply to a note from the new government of Russia requesting that they abide by the principles of the Decree on Peace. In truth there was little reason for them to believe that the Bolsheviks and their Left SR partners were anything more than a temporary government. On 26 November, therefore, less than three weeks after the uprising that brought them to power, the Bolsheviks decided to broach the idea of a separate peace treaty with the Germans. A delegation led by A.A. Yoffe was sent to the headquarters of the German Eastern Front at Brest-Litovsk (today simply known as Brest, a western border town in Belarus), arriving one week later. To demonstrate the broad makeup of the new government, the Bolshevik delegation was composed of a representative from each stratum of the population (a soldier, sailor, worker, etc.), with the peasant delegate being collected *en route*.

It is not hard to imagine the contempt with which they were received by the German High Command. The aristocratic Prussians, flushed with victories that had seen the German army complete its occupation of Russian Courland, Lithuania and Poland, could not comprehend the optimism of the Soviet delegation and were bemused by the bedraggled appearance of the Russian representatives. The Central Powers were led by Foreign Minister Richard Von Kuehlmann, the imposing Chief of Staff of the Eastern Front, General Max Hoffmann, and the Foreign Minister of Austria, Count Ottokar Von Czernin. No sooner had the Bolsheviks arrived than they began declaring that all territory occupied during the war should be returned to the previous owner, that there should be no indemnities, and that there should be self-determination by referenda in areas under dispute.

The Bolsheviks did not seem to be in a position to take any initiatives in this process, but they had an inflated sense of their own importance. Trotsky in particular considered that a workers' revolution was imminent, and thus it was in the best interests of the Soviet government to delay the peace process as long as possible [54]. Shortly, it was felt, Germany's position would be weakened and it would be forced to come to terms that were in line with Bolshevik requests. However, the Soviet suggestion of a six-month armistice was rejected. After some initial difficulties, the Germans accepted a Soviet proposal that the troops that would be available to the German High Command following an Eastern Front peace treaty should not be transferred to the Western Front. This request demonstrates that at this stage, the Bolsheviks were very concerned with the allies' reaction to Russia's withdrawal from the war. On 15 December, therefore, an armistice was signed by the Central Powers (Germany, Austria-Hungary, Turkey and Bulgaria) and Soviet Russia for a four-week period, with a proviso that either side must give a seven-day warning of any intention to break it.

An additional problem for the negotiators at Brest-Litovsk was the attitude of the Entente. On 8 January President Woodrow Wilson issued a peace proposal of 14 points, somewhat similar to the ideas put forward by the Bolsheviks but failing to recognize the new Russian government. The Central Powers refused to adhere to such terms. On the next day, when the talks at Brest-Litovsk were resumed, General Hoffmann dispensed with formalities, spread out his map, and demanded that the Germans be given some 150,000 square kilometres of territory that had belonged formerly to the Russian Empire. It included the Baltic states other than a portion of Estonia, Poland, and territories of eastern Galicia inhabited for the most part by Ukrainians, Jews and Belarusians. The shocked Bolsheviks asked for an adjournment of ten days to consider German demands.

Once again the question of Ukraine had to be dealt with. By this time Trotsky had replaced Yoffe as head of the Soviet delegation, and Trotsky was furious when a delegation from the Ukrainian Central Rada arrived in Brest-Litovsk to negotiate separately with the Germans. The Central Rada had proclaimed the independence of Ukraine on 22 January 1918. Fighting continued in Ukraine between a mainly Russian Bolshevik faction and the forces of the Rada. On 9 February the Bolsheviks managed to capture Kyiv, after which the German High Command, frustrated by the delaying tactics of the Bolsheviks and – not least – the tendency of the Soviet delegation to deluge the troops of the Central Powers with propaganda leaflets, decided to support the Central Rada and assisted the Ukrainian government militarily. Shortly afterwards, the Bolshevik troops were forced to retreat to their main base, the Ukrainian capital of Kharkiv. Thereafter, the German army controlled the situation in Ukraine, further weakening the Bolshevik position at the peace negotiations [101; 103].

During the ten-day recess to discuss the German territorial demands, three distinct factions emerged within the Bolshevik committee. Lenin, with a small group of followers, was insistent that the proposals be accepted. As usual, he put his thoughts to paper with a pamphlet entitled *Theses on the question of the immediate conclusion of a separate and annexationist peace*. Practically minded, Lenin felt that there was no choice but to accept the demands since the Bolsheviks had no army and no wish to continue the fighting. The entire country needed some breathing space and must concentrate on enemies within. A second group supported the idea of a revolutionary war against the imperialist Central Powers, somewhat akin to the French revolutionary army of the late eighteenth century. This group was led by 'left' Bolsheviks, such as Nikolay Bukharin and Karl Radek, and had the backing of the Left SRs. According to one account, it had the support of 32 out of the 63 delegates in the Central Committee [53]. If this was the case, then some of that support must have been weak, since it was a third notion that was eventually accepted.

A middle group led by Trotsky came up with the novel, though naive notion that the Bolsheviks would lay down their arms and refuse to take any further part in the war, but they would not sign a peace treaty based on the terms dictated by General Hoffmann. They would simply walk out of the talks. Though Bukharin's group was the largest, Lenin seems to have resolved on a tactical alliance with Trotsky. The latter's solution was also a continuation of the delaying tactics employed by the Bolsheviks from the outset. When talks recommenced at Brest-Litovsk on 30 January, the Soviet delegation managed to protract them for a further ten days before the frustrated Germans gave them an ultimatum. At that point, on 10 February, Trotsky put his theory of 'No peace and no war' into operation, and the Bolshevik delegation departed from Brest-Litovsk. A tense period followed for the Russians as they waited to see what the German reaction would be.

One week later, the German army resumed its advance eastward. Indeed there was little to stop them. The Russians retreated without even destroying bridges or taking other measures that would slow the German assault. On 18 February the cities of Lutsk and Dvinsk were occupied. The capital itself seemed under threat, such was the rapidity of the German march and the lack of resistance. On 17–18 February the Bolshevik Central Committee met again. Lenin was now frantic. For a brief time he remained precariously in a minority, but ultimately Trotsky decided that the German danger to the new Soviet state was too great to ignore. An urgent message was sent to the Germans communicating the Bolshevik decision by radio. It was unheeded for three days and the advance continued.

This moment is important because in retrospect it was the most critical period for the future of the new Soviet state. Frantic preparations were made to defend Petrograd. The duplicity and weakness of the Bolsheviks was especially evident in a request to the abandoned western allies for assistance. A decree, 'The Socialist Motherland is in Danger!', was issued. This time the danger emanated not from a feeble Kornilov but from the most efficient and powerful army in Europe. On 23 February, however, the Germans sent the Bolsheviks new demands that they should retain all the territories occupied in the five-day advance, in addition to several humiliating proposals. Soviet Russia was to lose all three Baltic states, Poland, the majority of Belarus, and was forced to remove all troops from Finland and Ukraine. It would have to accept the Central Rada as the legitimate government of Ukraine and cede territories in the south to the Turks. Russia would not be permitted an army and would have to pay a heavy indemnity to her conquerors. These terms had to be agreed to within two days [53]. Meanwhile the German advance continued and the city of Pskov fell to the Germans on 24 February.

Once again the Bolsheviks had to make a critical decision. Lenin threatened to resign if the proposals were not accepted. In truth the Bolsheviks had little choice if they wished to remain in office. The Soviet Executive Committee supported the conclusion of the Bolshevik Central Committee and the German proposals were accepted by 116 votes to 85, with 26 abstentions. On 1 March the respective delegations returned to Brest-Litovsk – but with the absence of Trotsky, who would not have lowered himself to accept such terms in person – and the treaty was signed two days later. In between the Bolshevik arrival and the finalization of the treaty, German planes dropped bombs on Petrograd, an event that caused hasty preparations for the removal of the government and ministries to Moscow. The Bolsheviks lost one-third of the former empire's population, more than half of its industrial enterprises and critical supplies of coal and iron ore. The Treaty of Brest-Litovsk remains as the twentieth century's most extreme example of a dictated treaty. The western allies, and particularly the United States, saw it as a complete negation of the ideas of Woodrow Wilson. When the Germans were forced to concede defeat on the Western Front in November 1918, the measures applied against them at Versailles were much harsher than they might have been as a result of Brest-Litovsk.

Lenin had got his way and an argument can be made that the Treaty of Brest-Litovsk constituted a temporary retreat, a skilful move to buy the Bolsheviks time to consolidate their new state. This view, however, gives Lenin more credit than he deserves. The Bolsheviks may be commended for the initial armistice, but their leaders badly misjudged the situation and the German reaction. It might have been possible to avert catastrophe by signing a treaty as early as possible. There was no other way. The eventual outcome of the treaty was the end of the first Soviet government. Though the ensuing Fourth All-Russian Extraordinary Congress on 14 March approved the treaty, the 283 Left SR delegates made known their displeasure. The next day, the SR ministers withdrew from the Council of People's Commissars and the coalition government with the Bolsheviks was ended. Just a few days earlier, on 11 March, Moscow had been formally proclaimed as the new capital of Soviet Russia. The border cities were no longer safe. Even long-term Bolsheviks were disgusted with the Brest-Litovsk treaty, which was far more humiliating than the Treaty of Portsmouth in 1905. Henceforth, the Bolsheviks would rapidly lose their domestic popularity, one that had been gained with misleading ease while in opposition. To maintain power – Lenin's primary goal – it would be necessary to use force.

THE WOMEN'S QUESTION

The women's question was rarely at the forefront of Social Democratic thought in the period prior to 1917, mainly because the prospects of success seemed so remote as to render such issues meaningless. The Russian Social Democrats had a strong belief that the institution of the family was connected with the old order, and that when this order collapsed, the family would disappear as an institution. Such beliefs could hardly be stated openly during the revolutionary upheaval of 1917 because they would have alienated the bulk of the population. Lenin was quite willing to embrace the plight of women in Russian society as a theoretical issue. From 1908 onward, the party had a women's section and one of Lenin's quotes from this period was that 'We must win over the millions of women to fight for our cause'. In 1917 a Bolshevik women's newspaper was issued called *Rabotnits'* (female worker). Lenin's main concern, however, was to establish a tightly knit and cohesive party organization. In his view the women's issue was secondary to that of a conflict of the classes [83].

Several women played a prominent role in the Russian Social Democratic movement. One of the earliest figures was Vera Zasulich, a close colleague of Plekhanov and Akselrod in the Russian emigration in the latter part of the nineteenth century. Zasulich had shot and seriously wounded General F.F. Trepov, the police chief of St Petersburg, in January 1878, and subsequently been acquitted at a famous trial. She was one of the founder members of the first Marxist group and carried out her work for the most part in western Europe. A closer associate of Lenin was the French-born revolutionary Inessa Armand, who grew up in Moscow before returning to Paris during the First World War. Armand came back to Russia with Lenin in April 1917 and became the leader of the women's section within the Central Committee of the party. Armand was a firm believer that the role of the family had to be changed under the new Soviet regime.

The best known of the Bolshevik feminists, however, is Aleksandra Kollontay, an idealistic radical who had maintained from the outset that a socialist revolution would lead directly to the liberation of women. Born in 1872, the daughter of a general from Ukraine, she joined the Bolshevik faction of the Russian Social Democratic Party directly in 1906. Though she also left Russia in 1908, she returned in 1917 and became a member of the Executive Committee of the Petrograd Soviet later in that year. Kollontay took part in both the Bolshevik uprising and the Second Congress of Soviets, at which she was voted a member of the presidium. In 1919 she published a pamphlet entitled *New Morality and the Working Class*, which was a propagandistic advocacy of free love (a subject elaborated in her 1925 book, *Free Love*). Kollontay considered that the act of sexual intercourse was no more meaningful than consuming a glass of water, a statement that caused some of the more moralistic Bolsheviks, such as Lenin, to shudder. She was soon to fall foul of the increasingly bureaucratic Bolshevik leadership, however, and eventually was appointed the Soviet ambassador to Norway, a convenient method of removing her from the political scene.

What were the goals of radical Russian women? How did their position in society compare with that of their western European counterparts? By 1917 Russian women were relatively well represented in various career sectors, making up about a quarter of educational and medical staff. In the Russian countryside, female doctors were more common than males. Women had also been prominent in the nineteenth-century revolutionary movement while also developing cooperative and similar organizations in rural regions. Though women can be said to have started the revolution of March 1917 with a march for bread, they did not so do in pursuit of gender aims. Nonetheless, after the success of the March Revolution, activists established a Union for the Equal Rights of Women, which advocated the enfranchisement of women, the right to divorce, and maternity leave. The relationship between such movements and the Kerensky government was quite positive.

In April 1917 this Union was divided. Bolshevik women such as Armand abandoned the Union on the grounds that they were more concerned with class than with gender issues. Most women in the Bolshevik movement were prepared to subordinate their views on women's rights or the role of the family to the more immediate concern of unity within the working-class movement. In short, the Bolshevik Party was so tightly disciplined that prior to the November Revolution, it was not prepared to give free rein to women's issues. The latter were secondary even though there were individual spokespersons, most notably Kollontay, who were more demanding and forthright. In November 1917 there was reason for women to hope that their goals would be dealt with by the new government [83]. The early achievements of the Bolsheviks in this regard were not negligible, though many were of short duration.

Thus by late 1917, women were permitted to keep their jobs during and after pregnancy; they could easily get divorced on their own initiative; special measures were taken to safeguard the rights of single mothers; and there was active discussion about raising the wages of women to the level of men's [76]. Women could vote and in virtually all respects their political rights were equal to those of men. Kollontay wanted to go further, advocating 'free love' and the eventual elimination of the family unit. On 20 December 1917 religious marriages were abolished and the church no longer had the right to register a marriage. Subsequently it became a matter of choice whether a union need even be registered, excepting cases when there was a dispute over which partner should have custody of a child. Abortion became legal under the Bolshevik government and birth control was endorsed also. For a brief time the views of the party and the women's movement converged on the subject of communal nurseries and clinics for children. Many Bolshevik feminists felt that children could be raised outside families and under the influence of the party. To some extent, these views were put into practice in the concept of pioneer camps and the Komsomol (young Communist) movement.

This idealistic society, which expressed at least some of the goals of the women's movement in Russia, was short-lived. The Bolsheviks were essentially a minority in power constantly fighting battles against their more numerous enemies. They could retain power only through terror (see below), and through the creation of a massive and all-pervasive party bureaucracy. A gap soon emerged between Lenin and Trotsky, on the one hand, and rising bureaucrats who were more dependent on the creation of a broader structure, such as Stalin and Molotov, on the other. New party functionaries were recruited from the more backward sectors of society: rural peasants, for example, flocked to the towns and had not the faintest notion of issues such as women's rights. Further, from the beginning, women were grossly underrepresented in the government structure. They made up 5.4 per cent of members of the Moscow Soviet in 1917, for example, and even lower percentages in the first Soviet government. Women made up about 12 per cent of all party members, however, and higher percentages among Russian Bolsheviks.

Few of the gains of the revolution stood the test of time. By the time of Lenin's death in January 1924, a more conservative trend was in evidence within the Soviet government. Marriage was once again registered and widely accepted. The family not only did not disappear, it solidified under the Stalin regime. Kollontay and her supporters became part of what was termed the Workers' Opposition, formed in 1920 (the main goal of which was to preserve the independence of trade unions against Trotsky's wish to incorporate them into the state structure) [20]. In the entire history of the Politburo, which was to emerge as the leading organ within the Communist Party hierarchy, only one woman was ever appointed a member of it (in the Khrushchev period, as Minister of Culture). Non-Russian groups, particularly from the Muslim republics of Central Asia, denied women virtually any role in the political process. In a sense, however, prominent Bolshevik women paved the way for this state of affairs by their willingness to sacrifice their ideals for the cause of the party. Once that party took power, and after the initial euphoria, traditional Russian values were reinstituted. Even Lenin at heart possessed innately bourgeois views on the family (though he had no children himself) and was alienated from the more radical of the women's demands [76]. The Russian Revolution then did not result in the liberation of women.

UTOPIA IN POWER

The Bolsheviks were anxious to put many of their principles into place as soon as they had their hands on the reins of power. On 11 November an eight-hour working day was introduced throughout the areas of Russia that they held. By the end of the month, it was announced that all those enterprises that employed more than five people would be subjected to 'workers' control'. In Petrograd the authorities founded an All-Russian Workers' Control Council, and no factories could be closed without the permission of this body. It proved more difficult to deal with private banks. Though the Bolsheviks took possession of the State Bank, they did not try to push through immediately the nationalization of banks, believing that they could use the existing system of private banks as a means of funnelling money into government coffers. This did not work and the Bolshevik leaders were soon grumbling that the bourgeoisie was attempting to sabotage the revolution by withholding funds.

On 27 December the banks in Petrograd were seized by the Red Guards. Banks were nationalized and all the private banks were joined to the main State Bank. On the same day, the Supreme Economic Council was created to organize and run the national economy. The main problem faced was that nearly half of the capital in the largest of the private banks was foreign-owned. Therefore, on 3 February 1918 the Bolshevik government annulled all the debts incurred by the tsarist government, a move that incensed Russia's former allies, particularly France. On 22 April the government took over all foreign trade, by which time it had complete control over the operation of the economy. It controlled the lives of its citizens in other ways too. On 5 February 1918 a decree separated the Russian Orthodox Church from the state and removed it from any role in the school system. The Russian calendar was changed from the Julian to the Gregorian so that it now coincided with that of the West.

In the regions, the Soviets of Peasant Deputies were gradually merged with the Soviets of Workers' and Soldiers' Deputies, and this process was completed during the spring of 1918. A slower but gradual process was the abolition of the city dumas and the zemstvo councils, which was completed only by the summer of 1918. The Bolsheviks had achieved administrative as well as political supremacy. They were in a position now to put their economic theories into practice and to begin to build up industry. However, the regime was far from secure, and would soon become preoccupied with the need to eliminate internal enemies and counter-revolutionary forces, both real and imagined. Lenin personally always felt insecure, trusting few people and suspicious of many. It was necessary therefore to create and develop an organ to defend the revolution that he had engineered.

THE CHEKA AND THE RED TERROR

During the existence of the Military Revolutionary Committee, a special section had existed within it to question those arrested as suspected counter-revolutionaries. On 20 December 1917 the Council of People's Commissars discussed the idea of transforming this section into a more permanent body. This organ was called the All-Russian Extraordinary Commission for the Suppression of Counter-Revolution and Sabotage (better known by its acronym – the Cheka) [*Doc. 14*]. Continuity was maintained by the appointment of the former head of the special section as chief of the Cheka, Feliks Dzerzhinsky, a Belarusian-born Pole who was fanatically devoted to the cause of the Bolsheviks and who was a man of impeccable personal morality (though it is difficult to assign the adjective moral to one who could inflict the death penalty so readily). Initially the Cheka was made up of a committee of eight, including Bolsheviks such as I.S. Unshlikht and Y.H. Peters, in addition to several Left SRs.

The stated goals of the Cheka were to prevent all counter-revolutionary activities and sabotage throughout the territory of Soviet Russia, and to put a stop to drunkenness, rioting in the streets, public demonstrations against the government, and all forms of banditry [*Doc. 14*]. The activities of the Cheka remained limited as long as the government was run from Petrograd. Once the Soviet regime was administered from Moscow, however, from mid-March 1918, the activities of the new secret police were intensified. In theory the Cheka was subordinated directly to the Council of People's Commissars, but in practice it could arrest and execute suspects without trial and without the permission, written or otherwise, of the Soviet government. Supporters or sympathizers of the young Soviet government have claimed that the Cheka was a necessary temporary instrument for the regime to defend itself against internal enemies. In truth, the Cheka needed little provocation to take action. The organization swelled as branches of the Cheka were created across the territory held by the Bolsheviks. Before long it had become a state within a state, subjecting its victims to gross tortures and committing atrocities that were a forerunner of similar organs later in the twentieth century (such as the German SS).

The first actions of the Cheka were directed against opposition groups in Moscow. On 12 April Cheka troops surrounded the known centres of Anarchism in Moscow and arrested their leaders. They also eliminated weak groups that were devoted to the removal of Bolshevik power: the Central Council of Strike Committees and a group of officers who had plans to form a military dictatorship. In these actions, several hundred people were arrested and punishments were sometimes mild. As the year progressed, however, penalties became more severe. Though the Bolsheviks had proclaimed the abolition of the death penalty, the Cheka obeyed no such rules. The situation became particularly acute because of the growing rift between the Bolsheviks and their former Left SR allies, who had become alienated by the signing of the Treaty of Brest-Litovsk and wished to provoke a new war with Germany in order to reverse the stipulations of that treaty. Matters were made more complex by the fact that there were many Left SRs in the Cheka, including in the leadership itself, and to a lesser extent in the soviets and the Red Army.

Though the Left SRs were not part of the Council of People's Commissars, they were still part of the Soviet Executive. Moreover, there was a new regrouping of political alliances in the spring of 1918 when elections were to be held to soviets across the country. Both the Mensheviks and SRs had gained in popularity since the Bolsheviks took power, and there was little to prevent an alliance with the Left SRs. The Mensheviks had even gained a foothold in the former capital of Petrograd, where they established an Assembly of Factory Delegates that encompassed many of the personnel who had been responsible for the Bolsheviks' surge to power a few months earlier. The brief period of Bolshevik rule had brought little benefit to those groups that had secured Lenin's party in power. After the Brest-Litovsk treaty, Soviet Russia was not officially permitted an army or navy. Unemployment had reached a massive scale, especially in those industries that had been reliant on supplying the army with weapons. In such a situation, it was hardly surprising that the Soviet elections of the spring of 1918 resulted in a resounding defeat for the Bolsheviks everywhere except Moscow. For a heady period it seemed that the slogan of 'All power to the Soviets!' might paradoxically be a means for the removal of Lenin and his party. Under these circumstances, Lenin was once again prepared to take any steps that would see his party remain in power.

The opposition could focus on the Brest-Litovsk treaty as the source of many of the country's troubles, severing as it did Moscow from the main industrial artery of the Donbass. Soviet Russia was left as a rump state with a government that no longer represented the population. But worse was to come. In late April, the Germans engineered a *coup d'état* in Ukraine, which saw the removal of the Central Rada and the installation of a wealthy landowner with virtually no popular support, General Pavlo Skoropadsky, as Hetman of Ukraine. Not only was this a sign of the restoration of land ownership in Ukraine, much of the grain surplus produced was to be used to feed the German army. The treaty therefore seemed to mean little. The western allies likewise felt that hostilities would soon be renewed between the Russians and the Germans. At the same time, Count Wilhelm Mirbach was named German ambassador to Russia and almost upon arrival in Moscow became the centre of speculation and rumours that his role was to install a puppet regime in Moscow also.

In May 1918, the Soviet government officially banned the Mensheviks and mainstream SRs from participation in the Soviet Executive Committee, thus leaving only the Bolsheviks and Left SRs with any decision-making authority (in reality real power had always lain with the Bolshevik Party rather than the organs of government). Support for the Left SRs had been growing as that for the Bolsheviks was decreasing. There was every indication that when the Fifth Congress was elected, they would hold a majority of seats. Lenin countered this possibility through the Committees of Poor Peasants (*Kombedy*) that had been created in the villages. In those centres where the soviets were anti-Bolshevik (probably the majority), the committees were permitted to appoint their own delegate. In short, these elections were carefully manipulated by the Bolsheviks to ensure that they held a majority at the Congress, a factor that prompted the Left SRs to try to overthrow the government, with the backing and collusion of the British and French.

In June 1918 the Left SRs officially declared their opposition to the Bolshevik government. On 6 July they made an abortive effort to seize power at the time of the Fifth All-Russian Congress of Soviets in Moscow. A Cheka official, Y. Blyumkin, managed to enter the Germany Embassy with forged papers, and shot and killed the German ambassador, Mirbach. Lenin, who had thrown in his lot with the Germans, subsequently had to apologise personally for this outrage, but the event did not spark a renewal of hostilities with Germany as the Left SRs had hoped. Nevertheless, the uprising was quite serious, mainly because the Bolsheviks had kept relatively few troops in Moscow. Troops supporting the Left SRs tried to arrest the Bolshevik delegates to the Congress, who had gathered at the Bolshoi Theatre. The majority of the workers, soldiers and sailors in the city, however, remained loyal to the Bolsheviks and the *putsch* failed. Thirteen Left SR leaders were executed, though their movement was not suppressed.

After this setback, the Left SRs continued the terrorist tradition of their Populist predecessors. A wave of terrorism struck Soviet Russia in the summer of 1918. According to the official Soviet account of the revolution, there were 414 terrorist attacks in July 1918 alone that resulted in the deaths of thousands of Soviet officials. Some occurred in the two major cities of Moscow and Petrograd. On 20 June V. Volodarsky, head of the Petrograd party association, was killed. On 30 August 1918 M.S. Uritsky, the prominent leader of the Petrograd Cheka and a longtime Bolshevik, was also assassinated. Lenin was scheduled to give a talk at a factory in Moscow that same day. On his way out, he was shot twice by a deranged SR, Fanya Kaplan, and seriously wounded. Though he recovered, the bullets were never removed and may have contributed to Lenin's feeble medical condition a few years later. The Bolsheviks connected these two events, though the timing appears to have been a coincidence. Lenin had rarely appeared in public prior to this time. Most Muscovites would not have recognized him in the street [53]. The assassination attempt prompted the Bolsheviks to deluge the populace with propaganda about the 'beloved leader' and the need to protect him. As a martyr, Lenin acquired a new-found popularity that was deliberately cultivated by the party.

On 5 September the Bolshevik government officially proclaimed a Red Terror in response to the attempt on the life of Lenin. A search began for 'traitors', 'spies' and 'wreckers', and some 500 people were executed initially in Petrograd alone for the assassination of Uritsky. The number of Cheka victims in this period is uncertain, but effectively it was the first application of mass terror to the population of the land held by the Soviet government. The official reason was that the workers' government and the workers' leader needed to be protected. But the latter had little say in how the Cheka operated. It became an organization out of control, feeding a frenzy of retribution and gross tortures. The country by this time had entered a phase of civil war, always blamed in official sources on the desire of the western allies to overthrow the new Soviet regime. But first and foremost the civil war was brought about by the determination of the Bolshevik minority to rule alone and to hold power by force.

RESULTS OF THE FIFTH CONGRESS

The Fifth Congress of Soviets is significant because it was the last Congress in which non-Bolsheviks were allowed a voice and in which there was general freedom of debate (despite the undemocratic way in which it was elected). There were, for example, 382 Left SRs present, in addition to a few members of other groups, and the 773 Bolsheviks in attendance were far from united [64]. Lenin's speech was greeted with some jibes from the audience. Prior to August 1918 he did not have the sort of respect he received subsequently. Many Bolsheviks remained dissatisfied with the result of Brest-Litovsk and some other facets of Bolshevik rule. The Congress issued the first Soviet Constitution (of Soviet Russia) and announced that the country was a republic ruled by the Soviets of Workers', Soldiers' and Peasants' Deputies. The Constitution espoused world socialism as the ultimate goal and embraced the cause of the workers. Everyone was obliged to give their labour to the state, but workers and peasants were guaranteed free non-religious education, the right to bear arms, and freedom of assembly. The Soviet state controlled all natural resources of Russia as state property.

The Soviet state declared war on all exploiters. The exploitation of man by man was 'abolished' whether by former tsarist police, the clergy, all those related to the Romanov family (then under house arrest near Tobolsk in Siberia), or those who hired labour. The Constitution, however, was misleading and in some respects little more than a propagandistic decree issued with the intention of appealing to foreign workers. The Bolshevik Party was not even mentioned. The country, it was declared, was run by soviets. Anyone over 18, who gave their labour to the state, whether male or female, could participate in elections to the soviets. The supreme legal authority was declared to be the All-Russian Congress of Soviets, but the franchise was far from democratic as it was prejudiced in favour of urban areas. Whereas 25,000 city workers could elect one deputy, it took five times that number to elect a deputy from rural regions. Similarly, although the Soviet Executive Committee made decisions in between the convocation of congresses, it was controlled by leading Bolsheviks, who took their guidance from the Council of People's Commissars. The Soviet Constitution of 1918 was a façade because it concealed the real authority of the party and produced the appearance of a state run by soviets. It set a pattern for future constitutions, particularly the Stalin Constitution of 1936.

CHAPTER FOUR

THE CIVIL WAR

THE FORMATION OF THE RED ARMY

Perhaps the main reason why the Bolsheviks were able to come to power was by taking advantage of the great mutiny of the Russian army with promises to end the war and give out land to peasants returning to their villages. Order No. 1 symbolized the collapse of all authority in the Russian army, and the defeat of the Kerensky offensive in July 1918 solidified the disillusionment of the rank-and-file soldiers. But the Bolsheviks' precarious hold on power ensured that an army would be needed for survival. The decision to construct a new army was taken on 23 February 1918, even before the Brest-Litovsk treaty was signed with the Germans. In fact, it was precisely the continuing German advance prior to the final signing and the battles around Pskov (which changed hands twice) and defence of Petrograd that necessitated hasty preparations. Initially, the new army was based on volunteers, especially common criminals. Trotsky, the Commissar for War, wanted to build a worker army, but early results were not significant. The new recruits lacked training, discipline and weapons. Moreover, there were not enough of them.

Trotsky, with Lenin's backing, decided to recruit former officers of the tsarist army, a move that seemed tantamount to employing the class enemy. How were such officers to be trusted? First of all, the Bolsheviks restored army discipline and the stipulations of Order No. 1 were quietly shelved. Second, the Bolsheviks applied the harshest of tactics. The officers would find that their loyalty was necessary if their families were to survive. Only those with families living on Soviet territory were to be commissioned. Political commissars were recruited to keep watch for any signs of treachery or lack of diligence on the part of the officers. If officers refused to join the new Red Army, they would be given hard labour. In truth many were only too happy to join an army because they were lacking other means of subsistence. They fell under the jurisdiction of a Military Revolutionary Council that took orders from the Central Committee of the party. Once soldiers were on the battlefield, trenches of gunners were usually formed behind the

Soviet front to cut off the path of any who decided to retreat. The Red Army then was initially built on coercion and brute force, with the main recruitment campaign in the autumn of 1918 [106]. The vast majority of its officers came from the tsarist army, the numbers of which were between 50,000 and 75,000. At the peak of the civil war in 1919–20, the Red Army numbered some 5 million troops, a significant achievement that owed much to the organizational abilities of Trotsky.

OUTBREAK OF CIVIL WAR

The outbreak of civil war in Russia was made extremely likely by the dictatorial actions of Lenin's party. Its origins, however, are complex, and linked to the First World War, and the Entente's fear that military bases and supplies could fall into the hands of the Central Powers following the Treaty of Brest-Litovsk [116]. Accordingly, the event often cited as marking the first step in the war was the British decision to land troops at Murmansk in March 1918. This was not an attempt to remove the Bolsheviks from power. On the contrary, the Murmansk Soviet appears to have welcomed the arrival of the British and French. In early April, Japanese and then British troops landed in Vladivostok. The Japanese motives appear to have been predatory, namely to capture land in the Far East during a period of Russian weakness and allying themselves with local warlords operating in the Far Eastern territories. In contrast to the western powers, the Japanese were not suffering from war-weariness and posed a serious threat to Russian control over this region. In May, US troops reluctantly landed at Murmansk to join their allies, but with a mandate to take defensive measures only.

The situation changed dramatically because of the activities of the Czech Corps, some 60,000 well-trained troops who had initially been enlisted into the Austro-Hungarian army and captured during the fighting with the Russians. The Russians permitted them to form their own units in the allied cause, but prominent Czechs, particularly Thomas Masaryk, requested that the Corps should fight on the Western Front against the Germans, envisaging the troops as the foundation stone of the new state of Czechoslovakia that was to be formed after the collapse of the Austro-Hungarian Empire. On 18 March 1918 the Bolshevik government agreed to the western allies' request that the Czechs could return home. The allies wanted the Corps to return via the northern port of Arkhangelsk, but the Bolsheviks ordered that they should travel by train across the country to Vladivostok, and by April, trains carrying the Czechs and Slovaks began the journey to the east.

At this time, there was no clear indication of a decisive break between the Bolshevik regime and the Entente. Indeed until mid-May it seemed quite likely that the Bolsheviks and the western allies might find common cause against the Germans. Small-scale fighting had taken place in Ukraine and had seen the Bolsheviks and the Czechs Corps – based in Kyiv initially – fighting together against the Central Powers. Trotsky appears also to have envisaged that war with the Germans might continue, despite the stipulations of Brest-Litovsk. Lenin, on the other hand, decided that it was preferable to leave the Germans in control of Ukraine and make further agreements with them that would see extensive trade between the two countries. In this vein, Lenin's government made a decisive break with the western allies, rejecting any possibility of an alliance on 13 May 1918 [116]. From that point onward, the Entente's attitude to Soviet Russia changed, and the Czech Corps took on new importance, particularly as it constituted the only professional army on Russian territory at this juncture.

Once the Soviet regime had made its decision to maintain the link with the Germans, despite the latter country's virtual colonization of Ukraine, then both Trotsky and Stalin began to demand that the Czech Corps be disarmed. In Chelyabinsk, a skirmish broke out when the train carrying members of the Corps stopped aside a train carrying Hungarian prisoners of war. Several members of the Czech Corps were imprisoned by the local soviet, whereupon their fellow soldiers freed them and virtually took over the town. It became clear that Bolshevik control over the towns along the Trans-Siberian Railroad was fragile and Trotsky used this incident as an example to show that the Czech Corps could not be trusted. Yet by demanding that they relinquish their arms, Trotsky very much forced the issue, and the Czechs by June had begun to take over various towns, including Samara, Chelyabinsk, Omsk, Tomsk and Penza. They began to make common cause with disgruntled SRs, whose political outlook was not dissimilar to their own.

The Czech-Slovak rebellion fuelled the cause of the anti-Soviet activists, and soon several anti-Soviet governments were established in captured towns. The Bolshevik position in the summer of 1918 looked precarious. Soviet authorities were being removed from towns in quick succession. In June 1918 a government was formed in Samara called the Committee of Members of the Constituent Assembly, composed mainly of SRs (as a consequence of which Lenin expelled all SRs and Mensheviks – who had not taken any steps against the Bolsheviks – from local governments held by Soviet Russia). In Omsk there was formed a Western Siberian Commissariat, which received some support from the Entente powers, who by this stage were debating which of the anti-Soviet forces should be officially backed. A Regional Government of the Urals was formed in Yekaterinburg that included members of the Kadets, SRs, and Mensheviks [114]. German and Turkish troops occupied Georgia and Armenia. An army under General P. Krasnov and made up mainly of Cossack troops was formed in the Don region and began to march toward Tsaritsyn. Finally at the end of July, British troops entered Baku.

Though civil war had now broken out in earnest, there was no clear goal on the allied side. The Entente powers were anxious to maintain a viable force on the Eastern Front against the Germans, but there was for some time no consensus regarding which of the plethora of forces emerging against the Bolsheviks should receive their support with funds and arms. In the North Caucasus, a Volunteer Army founded in late 1917 by General Mikhail Alekseev and General Lavr Kornilov, but led after their deaths by General Anton Denikin, initially received support. After November 1918, however, with an armistice in the First World War, the goal of an Eastern Front had become unnecessary. At this stage, the allies might most wisely have pulled out of Russia altogether. But there were some politicians, most notably Britain's Lord of the Admiralty Winston S. Churchill, who felt that the world could not allow the survival of the Bolshevik regime. They decided to give their backing to Admiral A.V. Kolchak once it became clear that left to themselves, the various forces among the Whites would be unlikely to unite of their own volition [112; 116].

Kolchak's army was based in western Siberia and numbered around 250,000. Because Kolchak acknowledged that the Russian government should not renege on its debts to the western allies, he was regarded as the most acceptable figure for the future Russian leader. The allies provided him with sufficient funds for a major campaign in the spring of 1919. Denikin, with French backing, marched northward through Ukraine at the same time. From Arkhangelsk, where the British and Americans had established a base in August 1918, General E.K. Miller's army began to move southward, while a further army was located in Estonia under the command of General N.N. Yudenich. On paper these White armies looked formidable, but the question was how to coordinate activities. The Bolsheviks in turn operated their Red Army through a Revolutionary Military Council of the Republic (RMCR) formed in September 1918 and Soviet Russia was placed under martial law. The leading figure in the RMCR was Trotsky, who used his personal train to travel to various parts of the front.

UKRAINE AND OTHER NON-RUSSIAN TERRITORIES

On 9 February 1918 the German High Command and the Austro-Hungarian Empire had signed a separate treaty with the Ukrainian People's Republic, which recognized Ukraine as an independent republic. The disputed Kholm territory, which was claimed by Poland, was given to the new Ukrainian state, while the western regions of Galicia (Halychyna) and Bukovyna were to be given special language privileges within the Austro-Hungarian Empire. Ukraine, in return, was to serve as the granary of the German army, and was ordered to place all surplus food supplies at the disposal of the armies of the Central Powers. In reality, the supplies demanded cut into the subsistence needs of many farmers, and the decision-making authority for the amount of food allotted to the armies lay with the German High Command. It was promptly set at no less than one million tons.

Because they had achieved such a strong position in the east, and particularly in grain-rich Ukraine, the German High Command was not willing to take a neutral role in the political events of the time. In particular, the Germans were opposed to a Bolshevik takeover of Ukraine. After the signing of the Brest-Litovsk treaty on 2 March, the 'Soviet Ukrainian' government at Kharkiv was forced to dissolve itself on 14 April 1918. The Central Rada took advantage of the situation to return to Kyiv accompanied by a Sich Sharpshooters military group that had been organized by Evhen Konovalets and Andriy Melnyk. The German leadership, however, had become opposed also to the Rada, which it did not consider strong enough to guarantee continued grain supplies to the German army, and which was opposed by many sectors of the rural community.

On 28 April, therefore, on the orders of the German omnipotentiary in Ukraine, General Wilhelm Groener, the Central Rada was abolished. The Sharpshooters offered some token resistance, but generally the order was effectively carried out. The Germans already had a replacement regime in mind. Four days previously, Groener had met with Lieutenant-General Pavlo Skoropadsky, a prominent landowner, and the two had made plans to establish a new Ukrainian government. The general would be backed by the conservative group, the League of Landowners, a mainly Russophile group opposed to any manifestations of Ukrainian nationalism, and his government had the guarantee of the occupying military force, the German army. On this same day, Hetman Pavlo Skoropadsky was proclaimed the head of state.

The new regime had little real authority. The Ukrainian army was to be strictly limited in size. Any acts committed against German or Austrian soldiers were to be investigated in military courts. The Germans also had considerable influence over official appointments in the civil service, land commissions and other institutions. All Cabinet positions had first to be approved by the occupiers, who also performed jointly the function of border control of the new state. Ukraine was allowed to export grain or other raw materials but once again the needs of the German High Command took priority. Private landholding was decreed by law, a stipulation that earned the Skoropadsky regime the immediate antagonism of the majority of Ukrainians.

On 29 April 1918 Skoropadsky was proclaimed Hetman of Ukraine at an impressive ceremony at the St Sophia Cathedral in Kyiv. The title itself had not been used for 150 years, and no doubt through its usage the

Germans hoped to legitimize what essentially was a puppet regime. But was there an alternative government for Ukrainians? One should recall the relative weakness of the Ukrainian national movement and the fact that – as far as one can tell – the Central Rada had never commanded majority support among Ukrainians. Had this been the case, then Ukraine might have defended itself more ably against its external enemies. A situation of near anarchy had prevailed in the city of Kyiv, and the Central Rada had appeared powerless to control the situation. Moreover, Ukrainians constituted only a minority in almost all the municipal councils of Ukraine, and faced powerful anti-Ukrainian forces. The latter included both non-Ukrainians and those people who had been subjected to the processes of Russification under the tsarist regime. Such sentiments, as the present Ukrainian government has found, could not be eradicated overnight.

In addition, the city of Kyiv was somewhat isolated from what was happening elsewhere in Ukraine. What authority the Central Rada possessed, nonetheless, was based mainly in this city. Many laws issued in Kyiv could not be put into practice in the provinces because of strong opposition. Further, there were serious disagreements between the leaders of the Central Rada, particularly among the two principal Social Democratic figures, V. Vynnychenko and S. Petlyura, over what sort of Ukrainian state should ultimately be created. There were also divisions between the various political parties, and between Ukrainians and non-Ukrainians who lived in Ukraine. One can say therefore that there was no solid leadership of Ukraine. Whereas in Russia at this time, the political leaders were seasoned and mature individuals – Lenin, for example, was 48 – the leaders of the Central Rada were comparatively youthful and inexperienced. Even Vynnychenko was only 37; his successor Holubovich was 32; Doroshenko 35; and Petlyura 38. The noted historian Mykhailo Hrushevsky was more experienced at 51. The Ukrainian Social Revolutionaries were led by students. Many of them would indulge in endlessly protracted intellectual debates. What was lacking were leaders with organization or administrative skills during a period of crisis.

Hence one can assert that the Central Rada was doomed to failure in the same way as the Provisional Government of Kerensky in Russia. This period, nevertheless, provided a strong historical legacy, and the experience of the Central Rada was recalled during the events of August 1991. The reality, all the same, is that the Rada collapsed more from its own internal weaknesses than from the actions of any outside force such as the Bolsheviks. It was a bold attempt to govern Ukraine during a period of international upheaval. The events of the war and the October Revolution both assisted and impeded the progress of the Rada: its existence derived from the collapse of authority and army mutiny in Russia; while its fall was inevitable given its lack of mass support and the proximity and eventually dominant position in Ukraine of the German army.

Hetman Skoropadsky was a historical anomaly, a man who probably belonged in an earlier historical period. He was a direct descendant of Hetman Ivan Skoropadsky, who had been the chief of the Zaporizhzhyan Cossacks in the period 1709–22. He had also worked for the Russian monarchy as a personal aide to Tsar Nikolay II. The re-established Hetmanate proved short-lived and lasted only until the end of 1918. As the First World War came to an end, the German army began slowly to leave Ukraine. Without its support it was clear that Skoropadsky's tenure as head of state was limited. Vynnychenko and others feared that Skoropadsky was about to renew federal ties with Soviet Russia, and decided to make another bid to take over the country.

Their first step was to create a five-member Directory (reminiscent of Napoleonic France), which would rule a revolutionary government to replace the Hetmanate. Vynnychenko was appointed the president, and represented the Social Democrats, while Petlyura was also a member, as the representative of the Sich Sharpshooters. The pretext for the takeover by the Directory was the restoration by the Hetmanate of a regime that tolerated and supported the great landowners and which constituted a counter-revolutionary, reactionary regime. The Directory first met in Bila Tserkva, but initially found its path to Kyiv cut off by German troops. Until they left Ukraine, the Germans also regarded Petlyura and his troops with suspicion, and considered him a potential future dictator. Until they finally departed from Ukrainian territory, Skoropadsky was able to cling to power.

By 12 December, however, the Germans realized that there was little justification for remaining in Ukraine. Declaring themselves to be neutral in Ukrainian politics, they moved out of Kyiv. Two days later a Social-Democratic-inspired uprising ended with the establishment of a military government by the troops of Konovalets. Skoropadsky beat an ignominious retreat from the capital disguised in German uniform and made his way with his wife to German territory. The reasons for the collapse of the Hetmanate are clear. It was a weak regime that depended upon the military backing of the Germany army and lacked significant support among both the Ukrainians and non-Ukrainians in the proclaimed state.

Ukraine therefore had yet another government in the shape of the Directory. Though, as noted, there were technically five members of this organ, two of them effectively held power, and in their outlook and aims lay fundamental incompatibilities. Vynnychenko was an intellectual by nature, a socialist of profound humanitarian bent. By contrast Petlyura, with the backing of the Sharpshooters, exhibited strongly Russophobic tendencies and was determined to establish a Ukrainian state no matter what the cost. Russian-language signs were to be replaced with Ukrainian ones within three days, for example. This anti-Russian sentiment ruled out any possibility of cooperation with Soviet Russia. In fact, the Bolsheviks had begun to step up their own activities *vis-à-vis* Ukraine. On 17 November they had established a Provisional Workers' and Peasants' Government of Ukraine under Yury Pyatakov. The most influential figure in this planned regime was Kristian Rakovsky, a Romanian by birth, but a Bulgarian by citizenship, who had been a member of the first abortive Bolshevik government in Ukraine. To make the new regime a reality, the Bolshevik army began to advance into Ukraine in December 1918, led by Antonov-Ovseenko, Stalin and Zatonsky. In order to look at the background to this operation, let us look briefly at the position of the Bolsheviks in Ukraine in the year 1918.

The Bolsheviks in Ukraine had remained a tiny party that was uncertain over its future policy directions. In April 1918 an important party conference was held in Tahanrih. There, the Kyiv delegation of Bolsheviks, led by Mykola Skrypnyk, gained ascendancy over the Russian delegations, and established the Communist Party of Ukraine (CP[b]U) as an independent political party that was to have no organizational affiliation with the Russian Communist Party (RCP[b]). Yet two months later, when the First Congress of the CP[b]U was held in Moscow, this policy – perhaps inevitably given the geographical circumstances – was reversed. The Kyiv group found itself in open dispute with other factions, most notable of which was the Kharkiv–Katerynoslav group. Eventually the pro-Russian line was successful, but a strong nationalist opposition emerged within the Ukrainian Communist Party. It is important also to keep in mind that in the summer of 1918 only 7 per cent of party members were ethnic Ukrainians. In the meantime, the Directory was clearly divided in January 1919. One month later, the city of Kyiv had fallen to the Bolshevik forces. Vynnychenko had fled abroad and Petlyura took over the presidency of the Ukrainian National Rada (UNR) Directory. Over the next ten months a series of battles and skirmishes took place between nationalist and Communist forces.

The situation was complicated further by the situation in western Ukraine. There, on 1 November 1918, as a result of the collapse of the Austro-Hungarian Empire, Galician and Bukovynian Ukrainians declared the formation of a Western Ukrainian People's Republic (WUPR). Under the leadership of Yevhen Petrushevich, it included territories of Galicia east of the San River, the Lemko region of the far west, and Ukrainian-populated parts of northern Bukovyna and Transcarpathia. The WUPR troops fought against both the Red Army and subsequently the Russian White Army of General Anton Denikin. The situation was confused further by the presence of significant Anarchist forces under Nestor Makhno, a colourful figure, who supported the UNR in most instances but was not averse to changing sides from time to time and fighting on behalf of the Bolsheviks.

Eventually the army of the UNR was trapped between the Bolshevik army to the east and the Polish army to the west. Consequently, it ended regular military functions on 4 December 1919, and resorted to guerrilla-type warfare. In April 1920 the Poles and the UNR made common cause against the Bolsheviks. Petlyura offered his assistance to a Polish invasion, and on 7 May Kyiv fell to the Poles and the Ukrainians. What was known as the Polish–Soviet war featured several dramatic turns. The Bolsheviks were able to reorganize their armies under S.M. Budenny and M. Tukhachevsky, and the Soviet counter-offensive took them across the entire territory of Ukraine to the outskirts of Warsaw. At that point, the French sent military advisors to the aid of the fledgling Polish state and the Polish army then once again occupied large sections of Right-Bank Ukraine. A truce was reached between Poland and Soviet Russia on 18 October 1920, one that could only augur badly for the UNR and its Directory, which now was once again trapped between two stronger powers. On 21 October UNR troops ended their conflict and were interned inside Poland.

The Russian Revolution fed a tide of separatist and independence movements among other former subjects of the Russian Empire. Russia's military defeat and the downfall of the monarchy, and the emergence of a Bolshevik regime that – officially at least – supported self-determination among nations, led to the loss of substantial territories. Finland, which had been part of the empire for over 100 years, was smarting over the Russification policies of the late nineteenth century, and was the first area to declare independence. After the end of the First World War, all three Baltic states – Lithuania, Latvia and Estonia – became independent. Early in 1918, Armenia and Georgia had done the same, though as noted, these states were subsequently occupied by the Georgian and Turkish armies. Perhaps the most contentious case of all was that of Bessarabia, which contained a substantial portion of Romanians, but had long been part of the Russian Empire. Initially, Bessarabia declared its independence early in 1918, but later in the year was joined with Romania, an action that the Russians never forgave and for which Stalin was to exact revenge in the summer of 1940.

REASONS FOR THE RED VICTORY

On paper, the advance of the various White armies in the spring and summer of 1919 would seem to have presented a formidable threat to the Bolshevik regime, particularly given western support, and with the formation of anti-Bolshevik governments in Asiatic Russia. The initial advance was that of Kolchak, who crossed the Ural Mountains in the spring with the intention of capturing Moscow. His advance was halted on the Volga, however, by the Red Army, which had superiority in numbers in this area. After the defeat, Kolchak's forces dissipated and he was captured by the Czech Corps, who passed him to the Bolshevik government in Irkutsk, where he was executed in February 1920. Denikin's forces in the south meanwhile advanced through eastern Ukraine in July 1919 and marched to within 250 kilometres of Moscow at Orel. The Bolsheviks desperately resisted this assault, and succeeded largely because Denikin had advanced faster than his supply bases in an effort to reach Moscow before the onset of winter. Once the attack had been repulsed, the defeat of Denikin turned into a rout. His forces retreated southward and ultimately came under the leadership of Baron Petr Wrangel in the Crimea, who was forced to evacuate the peninsula after some bold assaults on the mainland, only in November 1920. Wrangel is widely recognized as the most capable of the White Army commanders, but came on the scene too late to make a significant difference to the course of the war.

In the north, General Yudenich, armed with a few British tanks, came close to Petrograd in September 1919. The local party organization was led by Zinoviev, who appealed frantically for reinforcements, and the latter pushed back Yudenich's forces. Miller's attack also came to nothing. At crucial moments the Bolsheviks were able to rush reinforcements to the various fronts. They succeeded through a combination of organization and terror. Gradually the Bolsheviks began to recapture crucial strongholds of the former Russian Empire, including some of the territory that had been occupied by the Germans. In January 1920 both Tsaritsyn and Rostov-on-the-Don were reoccupied. By August 1920, a Bolshevik Southern Front, led by M.V. Frunze, had driven back the armies of Wrangel, whose forces were evacuated by French and British ships and taken to the Balkan countries in mid-November 1920. Almost simultaneously a truce was declared in the Polish–Soviet war (described above), followed by the Treaty of Riga, signed on 18 March 1921.

How were the Bolsheviks able to win the civil war? Perhaps the main reason was their control over the central heartland of Russia. They had a better system of communications, and controlled a considerable part of the industrial territories of the former empire. Factories in Petrograd and Moscow that had been harnessed to the war effort against the Central Powers could easily be redirected to the needs of the civil war. The Bolsheviks had better organization and, crucially, leadership [*Doc. 18*]. It is generally agreed that Stalin, the representative of the RCMR on various fronts, was more of a hindrance than a help and usually got involved in fractious disputes with local commanders and his nominal supervisor Trotsky. But Stalin's blundering did not entirely offset the general efficiency of Trotsky and his generals. In Budenny, Frunze, Tukhachevsky, and others, the Bolsheviks had an array of talent that was not matched by the White side.

The Whites in turn were divided as to overall leadership and goals. The armies of Denikin (especially) and Kolchak alienated the mass of peasants in their regions by their support for the former landowners. To many observers they represented the forces of the past. The White leaders had few political goals other than personal power, which would have resulted in a military dictatorship in some form or other. Their armies were plentiful but they were widely scattered over a vast territory. It was impossible for Kolchak, for example, to communicate effectively with Yudenich or Miller, separated from him by some 5,000 kilometres of territory. The troops of Denikin, who achieved some initial success, had conducted wholesale slaughter of the population (especially Jews) in the territories that they occupied. They were also impeded by the Anarchist troops of Makhno. Lastly, the support of the western allies was half-hearted, especially after the collapse of the Kolchak campaign. Both the French and the British faced a wave of domestic opposition to their involvement in Russia. France's only significant commitment was to the survival of an independent Poland.

The Bolsheviks ultimately had two additional advantages. The Whites could only be supplied by foreign powers and once that support was reduced, their armies faded away. Second, the civil war became at least in part a national struggle. Bolshevik propaganda emphasized the need to pre-serve Russia from outside enemies. The Bolshevik campaign for world revo-lution was temporarily subsumed by a rally to Russian patriotism. Even those who had little sympathy for the cause of the Bolsheviks could support such a campaign. The mass of peasantry, alienated by the disdain of the Whites for their goals, was thus happy to throw its support behind Soviet Russia. Lenin's regime was on a martial footing and the suffering of the population was acute. The casualties suffered during the Russian Civil War may have been three times as high as those during the First World War, though famine and disease caused many more deaths than the conflict itself. The highest estimate of the casualty toll is around 30 million.

WAR COMMUNISM

The period 1918–21 saw the imposition of a system known as War Com-munism. In part it fulfilled the objectives of the most ideological Bolsheviks, who felt that they could develop an economic system that was true to their Communist ideals. The system involved the nationalization of industry at a much more rapid rate than had originally been envisaged as a result of the civil war situation. About 80 per cent of all large industrial enterprises were in government hands by late 1919, and before the end of the following year the state had acquired most of the smaller industrial enterprises as well. The result was the creation of a vast bureaucracy under the auspices of the Supreme Economic Council, which simply lacked the means to run such a system and the officials of which had little experience. It has been noted that in Petrograd in 1918, one in four adults was a state official. Under workers' control, factory production plummeted. But the system was

1. Tsar Nicholas II and family.

2. World War I Russian trenches.

3. Lenin's arrival at Finland station.

4. The Bolshevik H.Q., October 1917.

5. Civil war – posing with skulls.

6. Trotsky and Red Army.

7. Red Army with dead comrades.

8. Trotsky c. 1919.

expanded further. By 1920, it was forbidden to own private property. House owners were dispossessed or forced to share their homes with several families. The state confiscated personal riches, and sums of cash were deposited by obligation into the state bank.

For the most part the state turned on the former privileged classes, the bourgeoisie. Wages and salaries were increasingly paid in kind, and money became increasingly superfluous. Some Bolsheviks anticipated that the state would be able to run a moneyless economy and that this was a natural progression from the establishment of a socialist regime. Money could be printed if and when it was needed. The key issues were twofold: the collapse of industrial output and the food question. As the government sought a reliable means of providing food for the workers, it turned on the peasantry. In the militant fashion that characterized his actions after taking power, Lenin introduced the concept of a class war in the countryside. His logic was that the most important grain-growing regions in the summer of 1918 were under the control of the Bolsheviks' enemies. The state therefore would ally with the poorer peasants against the rich.

In practice, this signified the formation of the Committees of the Poor Peasants (*Kombedy*) [*Doc. 16*], the goal of which was to requisition surplus grain from the rich peasants (*kulaks*) and middle peasants (*serednyaks*) [*Doc. 15*]. In May 1918 Lenin launched a 'crusade for bread' [*Doc. 17*] and the most serious assault began in the countryside in January 1919. The victimized peasants were quickly reduced to helplessness. Since many were paid their wages in kind rather than in rubles, the requisition of surplus grain took away their livelihood. The amount of land cultivated fell sharply, and the food supply to the towns began to fail. In turn, thousands of hungry workers flooded back into the countryside. City workers could find neither food nor jobs. Not all parties suffered. So-called 'bagmen' flourished: people who would bring food supplies to the cities and sell it on the black market. The Bolsheviks began to advocate the formation of cooperatives and collective farms, but very few were actually established. The grain requisitions, on the other hand, were brutally imposed [111].

The system of War Communism led to the almost total collapse of the Soviet Russian economy. Trade had ended and only the black market operated with any success. Yet to many peasants the alternative remained even worse: that of a return of the former landowners. Thus they were prepared to suffer War Communism as long as the civil war lasted and the future of Russia was in the balance. After the defeat of the Whites, however, Russia saw a series of peasant revolts on a massive scale. The largest was in Tambov, where some 50,000 peasants took part in an SR-led revolt, but there were also significant revolts in Ukraine, the Don and Volga regions, and others. Overpopulation in the villages and a dramatic fall in grain output led to widespread starvation that affected over 5 million peasants. In

1920–21 the Bolsheviks were obliged to appeal for outside help to offset the effects of famine, and the US Relief Administration led by Herbert Hoover responded.

As with the onset of civil war, much of the blame for the ills of War Communism lay with the Bolsheviks. Whereas Trotsky had used the skills of former tsarist officers in the new Red Army, the same practice was not applied to industry, where former managers and specialists were simply excluded from the production process. Similarly, those peasants who were most productive found themselves the victims of a regime that had characterized them as the class enemy. Though Stalin would take the assault on the kulak to new heights in the period 1929–33, the model was already in place under War Communism. Soviet Russia was in chaos, a starving country with no jobs, industrial production at a level that was less than half of that prior to the First World War, and in some industries (coal and steel are two examples) less than one-tenth. The towns were virtually depopulated. By March 1921, even Lenin had realized that changes had to be made and the system that embodied the ideals of many Bolsheviks ended.

THE KRONSTADT REVOLT

The rigours of War Communism and the food shortages had repercussions everywhere, including among the most fanatically pro-Bolshevik element in November 1917, the sailors of the Kronstadt naval base on Kotlin Island in the Gulf of Finland. By early 1921, few of these sailors had maintained their allegiance to the Bolsheviks, since the latter in their view had reneged on many of their promises. The sailors' views had become closer to anarchism. Rather than increased centralization of the economy and nationalization of industry, they preferred a federation of autonomous communes. They were also far from happy with the autocratic manner of Trotsky, the Commissar for War [*Doc. 20*]. But the spark that set off the revolt was the imposition of a new bread ration in March 1921. The crews of two warships mutinied and drew up a list of demands known as the Petropavlovsk Resolution, and began to form a breakaway republic that lasted for two weeks.

The demands of the sailors demonstrated their frustration with the 40 months of Bolshevik rule. Having founded their own newspaper, they also established a Provisional Revolutionary Committee and demanded that the socialist parties be accorded the rights they had had in 1917, such as the freedom of assembly and to issue their own publications. They opposed also Trotsky's mobilization of labour, which had decreed that workers be limited to specific jobs and locations. Above all, they wanted the removal of the grain requisition squads who had caused such problems in the countryside. The Bolshevik regime was also accused of failing to live up to the 1918

Constitution. Under their leader, S.P. Petrichenko, the sailors took over the Kronstadt base with the sort of euphoria not seen since the pre-civil war period. The Communist Party in Kronstadt became a powerless nonentity [109].

The Bolshevik regime immediately recognized the danger posed by this new revolt. With the civil war over, there was no longer any fear of foreign intervention, but the revolt of the sailors, whose exploits in the November Revolution had become legendary, was a serious embarrassment to the government. Trotsky delivered a high-handed ultimatum to the sailors, demanding that they at once give up all their weapons and surrender to the Soviet government. Not only did the sailors refuse, but the first Bolshevik assault over the ice from Petrograd was turned back with ease. Further assaults also failed. Only on 16–18 March, after 12 days of fighting, did the Red Army, with about 50,000 troops, succeed in subduing the rebel garrison. Once the base had been taken, the Bolsheviks acted ruthlessly, executing the leaders to a man. According to Trotsky, the Bolsheviks had put down a counter-revolution led by drunkards and hooligans. Lenin's reaction was more astute. He recognized that the regime had alienated those who had put it into power [*Doc. 21*]. The Kronstadt Revolt occurred in the aftermath of the civil war, but it symbolized the cruelty of the young regime that had begun on a wave of popular emotion but had constantly rejected compromise and moderation.

On 15 March 1921, as the final assault on the Kronstadt fortress was about to begin, the Tenth Party Congress meeting in Moscow introduced a complete reversal of economic policy. War Communism would be replaced by a new system that replaced grain requisitions on the peasantry by a tax in kind. Eventually this tax would be imposed in the form of money, and the result was that the peasants were free to dispose of their surplus grain once this flat tax had been paid. The new system was known as the New Economic Policy, a reversal seemingly of all that the Bolshevik regime had stood for. Capitalism would be returned to the village and even among small-scale industry. Those scholars and statespersons of the Gorbachev era who were sympathetic to Lenin maintained that this policy represented Lenin's real beliefs, and that War Communism had only been imposed as a result of warfare and the immediate need to preserve the Bolshevik regime.

The reality was precisely the opposite. War Communism had simply failed. Lenin recognized that if the Soviet regime were to be maintained, it would face a continuing and growing revolt in the rural regions [*Doc. 21*]. The Kronstadt Revolt was perhaps the crucial factor in the decision to change policy. The New Economic Policy had its supporters – the former Left Bolshevik Nikolay Bukharin was its chief advocate – but many of Lenin's associates were unhappy with what seemed like the relinquishment, however temporary, of true Bolshevik ideals. With the end of War Communism, the period of revolution came to an end. In December 1922 the four republics of Russia, Ukraine, Belarus and Transcaucasia would form a Union of Soviet Socialist Republics. The increasingly feeble Lenin – he would suffer a series of strokes beginning in 1922 – was at least able to prevail over his Commissar for Nationalities, I.V. Stalin, who had advocated federation of Soviet states within Russia. In theory, Russia was but one of four equal republics of the new USSR, but with the majority of the population and 75 per cent of the territory, this was never the case.

PART THREE   ASSESSMENT

CHAPTER FIVE

LENIN'S ACHIEVEMENTS AND FAILURES

Historians have long pondered over how a small minority party could have succeeded in obtaining and preserving its power in Russia and subsequently the Soviet Union. Among the critical factors cited are the popularity of the Bolsheviks in the autumn of 1917, the fact that they made promises that appealed to the broader population, the association of their rivals (the Mensheviks and SRs) with the government, and the unwillingness of the latter two parties to use the Soviet as a means to take power for themselves. This book has argued that the revolution very much belonged to Lenin even though he did not personally play an active role in the events of 7 November. It also maintains that the Bolsheviks in opposition were a very different party from the Bolsheviks in power. Prior to the November Revolution they were singularly attuned to the mood of the populace. Lenin in particular had an acute sense of timing, hence his constant spate of letters to the Bolshevik Central Committee in an effort to ensure that the moment did not pass.

In November 1917 the Provisional Government was on its last legs. Elections to the Constituent Assembly would presumably have gone ahead anyway, and it is highly unlikely that Kerensky could have retained his position as premier. The Bolsheviks also had a majority in both the Moscow and Petrograd soviets by this time. They could have played a decisive role in any socialist coalition government that might have been formed. However, Lenin never had any intention of sharing power. The increasing bureaucracy in the party was a direct consequence of the leader's overwhelming desire to rule alone and to remain in power, however unpopular they might have become. Logically a socialist revolution could not be reversed. Yet this was a socialist revolution that excluded the majority of socialists from a voice in decision-making. The first signs of what the future held were the Bolsheviks' arrogance and unyielding attitude in the Second Congress of Soviets and the January 1918 dissolution of the Constituent Assembly.

It could be argued that the outbreak of the civil war created the unity in the country that permitted the Bolsheviks to stay in office, that they could pose as defenders of the revolution in a struggle against the class enemy.

There is evidence to suggest, however, that the civil war itself was a direct result of Lenin's manoeuvring. Just as the Bolsheviks had ample opportunities to work alongside or share government with the other socialist parties, so also there were chances for them to continue in some form the alliance with the powers of the Entente. Germany had not only imposed a ruthless treaty on Soviet Russia, it had flagrantly interfered in the politics of former parts of the Russian Empire. In many respects, the war with Germany had not ended at Brest-Litovsk. At various stages in 1917–18, however, Lenin's relationship with the Germans was at best ambiguous. The Germans enabled him to return to Russia to foment revolution. It was Lenin who insisted on two occasions that German demands at Brest-Litovsk must be met; and it was Lenin again who preferred to make a deal with the Germans in May 1918 rather than work with the Entente, rendering the foreign armies protecting Russian military bases *ipso facto* hostile elements.

Did Lenin have a choice? The Bolsheviks after all faced almost overwhelming problems in 1918. The key factor was that in the long term, the democratic governments of the Entente could hardly have accepted the Bolsheviks as legitimate, let alone as allies. Winston Churchill was the most outspoken of western politicians, but there were many who abhorred the coming to power of a Marxist party. As the civil war demonstrated, the West would have preferred to see military dictatorship in Russia than Lenin's party in power. The Germans, on the other hand, might be content to use Ukraine as a supply base in collusion with a weak Russian government as long as the war continued. In May 1918 a defeat for Germany on the western front within six months looked improbable. From the Bolsheviks' perspective, on the other hand, a revolution in Germany was inevitable. Lenin and Trotsky felt that they could play for time in the knowledge that workers' revolutions would shortly occur throughout Europe. Russia would not be left alone as the sole socialist state.

After the failure of the uprisings in Berlin, Munich and Hungary, and the refusal of the Polish workers to support Tukhachevsky's assault on Warsaw in 1920, the goal of exporting the revolution had to be shelved. Instead, power at home needed to be consolidated through the ruthless suppression of internal enemies. In fact this process had begun early in 1918. At the Tenth Party Congress in March 1921, which introduced the New Economic Policy, a decree was also issued to ban factionalism in the party ranks. This decree was used thereafter to crack down on any wavering or dissension from the official party line. The Cheka already had its own empire and was to appear in new forms throughout the Soviet period. In addition, the ranks of officialdom had swelled to gross proportions. The Bolsheviks put the population into uniforms and gave them tasks.

In the countryside there had never been solid support for the Bolsheviks. The peasants were willing to tolerate a party that allowed them to divide up the land, but in the period 1918–21 they were themselves divided according to property, or whether they hired labour and could be categorized as kulaks. Once again, Lenin's party had a choice. It could have maintained the worker–peasant alliance that had been proclaimed. Instead it chose to rely on the worker while turning viciously on the peasant. Under War Communism the entire economy collapsed, and labour mobilization tactics deprived the Bolsheviks of key support in the cities, and at military and naval bases. The civil war had been won, but the costs had been horrendous and the suffering acute. Consequently, March 1921 constituted a temporary truce in the Bolsheviks' battle in the countryside. Whether it would have continued had Lenin remained in good health will always be a moot point.

Bolsheviks in power individually were also very different from Bolsheviks in opposition. The transformation from revolutionary to administrator or minister was almost impossible for some. Trotsky, for example, enjoyed his finest moments during times of crisis, when he could rally people with a speech or dash from one point to another. As a politician manoeuvring for power, he was (as Lenin remarked) clueless [*Doc. 21*]. Zinoviev and Kamenev had boldly stuck to their principles at critical times in 1917, opposing Lenin when they felt he was being too impetuous. By the summer of 1918 they had become sycophantic worshippers, only too anxious to develop a Lenin cult while their leader was still alive. This would grow to monstrous proportions after Lenin's death, but it was in place well before January 1924. The natural administrators, like Sverdlov (who died prematurely) and Stalin, thus came to the fore, and their path was made smoother by the party's tight discipline and centralization.

Lenin himself was the chief architect of this system. At various times he was prepared to take the most drastic punitive measures, to make an example of class enemies, or to order mass executions when milder instructions would have made little difference to the outcome. One such event was the execution of the Romanov family on 17 July 1918. In May 1918 Nikolay and Aleksandra had been moved to a house in Yekaterinburg. The Bolshevik leaders were debating whether to put the former tsar on trial – Trotsky envisaged himself in the role of prosecutor. Two months later it seemed that the city would be captured by the Whites and the Czech Corps. On the instructions of Yakov Yurovsky, a member of the Cheka who was in charge of the royal prisoners, the entire family was taken down to the cellar of the house and executed. Some of the children had to be bayonetted afterward. They were then taken to a disused mine shaft, soaked in acid and burned. It is now clear that this senseless execution was ordered by Lenin himself [68]. The tsar personally may have been considered a threat, though none of the White leaders sought to reinstall him in power. The children, however, and their bodyguards and servants, were completely innocent.

The massacre of the royal family was a typical indicator of the sort of ruler Lenin had become. This process did not begin in 1902, when he demanded a highly disciplined and centralized party. Lenin's pamphlet *What Is To Be Done?* remains a masterpiece of the strategy by which the party could take power, but it did not necessarily predetermine how the party would govern once in power. It revealed a flexibility within Marxism that would serve Lenin well. However, at every stage after the revolution, Lenin exhibited a chilling ruthlessness. Arguably it kept him in power, but it is also conceivable that much of it was unwarranted. Even after November 1917, there was a brief period when it appeared that some of the more utopian goals of socialism might be implemented. All these hopes – and some were expressed in the resolution of the Kronstadt sailors in March 1921 – were to be dashed over the next few years. By December 1922, when Lenin had the second stroke that curtailed his active participation in public life, the nature of the new state, the USSR, was already plain to see.

Nonetheless, the Russian Revolution continues to elicit some fervour and even romantic notions. At the time of writing there are plans to resurrect statues of Lenin and Stalin in different parts of Russia, and even to restore the statue of the first head of the Cheka, Feliks Dzerzhinsky, in the square outside the Lubyanka building in Moscow. In Moscow, Kyiv and Minsk (the latter two now capitals of independent countries), Communists remain a powerful force in public life. The day of revolution, 7 November, is seen as a time of hope, of ideas, of revolutionary activity, and of great leadership. The image of Lenin as a deity was attacked bitterly in the late Soviet period. Lenin's works, which made up an obligatory corner of every bookstore, were removed. And yet his image remains in Russia. It will not be erased by the end of the twentieth century. This small and shambling badly dressed figure, whose features were barely known to the Russian public until Fanya Kaplan tried to assassinate him, continues to fascinate statespersons, scholars and tourists alike. The democratic government of Boris Yeltsin could not take the ultimate step of removing Lenin's body from the mausoleum inside the Kremlin walls.

In one sense, those who feel that statues of Lenin should remain on display are right: 1917 was an epochal year for Russia, and there were times when Lenin and his party really did embody the feelings and hopes of the people, particularly the volatile masses in Petrograd and Moscow. The monarchy had fallen, but nothing stable had replaced it. The masses wanted a government that would follow their wishes, end the war, and provide them with food and land. The Bolsheviks were the only party that agreed to and fulfilled these wishes in any form. Ultimately, then, perhaps they failed to live up to early expectations because they were seduced by power. Thereafter everything that Lenin did was to ensure that his party remained the government, that all socialist rivals were excluded and in many cases outlawed. A siege mentality was developed of a state surrounded by enemies and bolstered by the real (somewhat half-hearted, especially in the case of the French and Americans) intervention of foreign powers on land that had formerly belonged to Russia. Only through repression and force could Lenin's party stay in office and these were the main characteristics of the early Soviet regime.

PART FOUR · DOCUMENTS

*The final months of the 1905 Revolution saw a widespread strike across
Russia. This letter from Tsar Nikolay II to his mother illustrates the tsar's
total lack of sympathy with or understanding of grievances of workers in
the capital. The tsar's first language was English.*

19 October, 1905.

My Dearest Mama – I do not know how to begin this letter. We have both
been through such grave and unprecedented events that I feel as if the last
time I wrote to you was a year ago. You remember, no doubt, those January
days when we were together at Tsarskoe – they were miserable, weren't
they? But they are nothing in comparison with what has happened now!

I am going to try to describe the position here as briefly as possible. A
month ago yesterday we returned from Transund, and the first fortnight
was comparatively quiet.

All sorts of conferences took place in Moscow, which Durnovo [P.N.
Durnovo, the Minister of the Interior] permitted, I do not know why. Everything was being prepared for the railway strike. The first one began in and
round about Moscow, and then spread all over Russia practically at once.

Petersburg and Moscow were entirely cut off from the interior. For
exactly a week today the Baltic railway has not been functioning. The only
way to get to town is by sea. How convenient at this time of year! From the
railways the strike spread to the factories and workshops, and then even to
the municipal organisations and services, and lastly to the Railway Department of the Ministry of Ways and Communications. What a shame, just
think of it! ...

God knows what happened in the universities. Every kind of riff-raff
walked in from the streets, riot was loudly proclaimed – nobody seemed to
mind. The governing bodies of the universities and the engineering schools
were granted autonomy but they do not know how to use it. They couldn't
even lock the doors in time to keep out the impudent crowd, and then of
course complained they could not get any help from the police – but do you
remember what they used to say in years gone by?

It makes me sick to read the news! Nothing but new strikes in schools
and factories, murdered policemen, Cossacks and soldiers, riots, disorder,
mutinies. But the ministers, instead of acting with quick decision, only
assemble in council like a lot of frightened hens and cackle about providing
united ministerial action.

When at various 'meetings' – that is the fashionable word nowadays [the
revolutionaries had adopted the English word 'meeting', but used it

exclusively in the sense of revolutionary meeting] – it was openly decided to proclaim an armed rising, and I heard about it, I immediately gave the command of all the troops in the Petersburg district to Trepoff [D.F. Trepov, Chief of Police]. I ordered him to divide the whole town into sections, with a special commander for each. The troops were ordered to use their arms immediately if attacked. This was the only way the movement or revolution could be stopped, because Trepoff made it quite plain to the populace by his proclamations that any disorder would be ruthlessly put down; and, of course, everybody believed that. So the ominous quiet days began, quiet indeed, because there was complete order in the streets; but at the same time everybody knew that something was going to happen – the troops were waiting for the signal, but the other side would not begin. One had the same feeling as before a thunderstorm in summer! Everybody was on edge and extremely nervous, and, of course, that sort of strain could not go on for long. Through all those horrible days, I constantly met Witte. We very often met in the early morning to part only in the evening, when night fell. There were only two ways open: to find an energetic soldier and crush the rebellion by sheer force. There would be time to breathe then but, as likely as not, one would have to use force again in a few months; and that would mean rivers of blood, and in the end we should be where we had started. I mean to say, government authority would be vindicated, but there would be no positive result and no possibility of progress achieved. The other way out would be to give to the people their civil rights, freedom of speech and press, also to have all laws confirmed by a State Duma – that, of course, would be a constitution. Witte defends this very energetically. He says that, while it is not without risk, it's the only way out at the present moment. Almost everybody I had an opportunity of consulting is of the same opinion. Witte put it quite clearly to me that he would accept the Presidency of the Council of Ministers only on the condition that his programme was agreed to, and his actions not interfered with. He and Alexei Obolensky drew up the Manifesto. We discussed it for two days, and in the end, invoking God's help, I signed. My dear Mama, you can't imagine what I went through before that moment; in my telegram I could not explain all the circumstances which brought me to this terrible decision, which nevertheless I took quite consciously. From all over Russia they cried for it, they begged for it, and around me many – very many – held the same views. I had nobody to rely on except honest Trepoff. There was no other way out than to cross oneself and give what everyone was asking for. My only consolation is that such is the will of God, and this grave decision will lead my dear Russia out of the intolerable chaos she has been in for nearly a year. The situation is very serious, in spite of the fact that I keep receiving declarations of very touching loyalty and thankfulness. The people seem to have gone mad – some from joy, others from discontent. The local administrations do not quite know how to act under the new regime – nothing is fixed yet – everything seems to be done by gentlemen's agreement. The very next day Witte found out what he was in for – many to whom he offered positions under him in one capacity or another now refused to accept. Old Pobiedonostseff [Konstantin Pobodonovtsev, the tsar's former tutor and Procurator-General of the Holy Synod] has resigned; his place will be taken by Alexei Obolensky. Galzoff has resigned too, but we have no successor for him as yet. All the Ministers are resigning and we have to find new ones, but Witte must see to that. At the same time it is essential to keep order in the towns, where loyal and hostile demonstrations are continually taking place and bloody clashes occur between them. We are in the midst of a revolution with an administrative apparatus entirely disorganised, and in this lies the main danger. But God Almighty will be our help. I feel Him supporting me and putting strength in me, which gives me courage and does not allow me to lose heart. I assure you we have lived years in these days, such torments, doubts, and indecisions. Your dear letter has just been brought to me, which you sent with Isvolsky. I thank you from the bottom of my heart, my dear Mama. I know you are praying for your poor Nicky. Our Saviour be with you! May God save and give peace to Russia. Yours with all my heart,

Nicky.

Edward J. Bing, ed., *The Secret Letters of the Last Tsar*, New York: Longmans, Green and
Co., 1938, pp. 182–6.

DOCUMENT 2   MILYUKOV ANALYSES THE SITUATION AFTER THE
1905 REVOLUTION

The historian Pavel Milyukov was to play a prominent role in the Russian Provisional Government's first Cabinet. His hostility to both the SRs and SDs is evident, as is his support for the establishment of a Duma so that Russia could make progress toward a more democratic state constitutionally rather than through revolution. The extract also describes the origin of the Fundamental Laws.

Each morning we read in the newspapers about workers' strikes in various Russian cities, and railroad employees, small artisans' groups, and unions from all sorts of professions were beginning to affiliate with the striking workers. The strikes were ever more frequently being described as 'general.' Alongside of the workers, the peasant movement also flared up – especially in the black-earth regions. Armed detachments of S.R.'s, now here, now there, committed acts of terrorism, directing their blows at all levels of the administration, from governors to neighbourhood and village police forces, at all ranks of the state police and gendarmes. One's eyes became used to the daily repetition of the same headlines, but it was difficult to perceive the dynamic of the revolution or to feel it from newspaper excerpts. Only later when these same facts were sorted out and classified in books was it possible to grasp the whole force of the revolutionary wave. The general meaning of the revolutionary outbursts was obscured by the absence of both a clearly expressed political direction and a unifying aim that would draw together various revolutionary outbursts motivated by the class demands of the workers, the local needs of the peasants, and so on. The socialist parties preferred to propagate general slogans rather than set concrete tasks. Systemic leadership from the center was not yet in evidence. According to the most revolutionary parties, the revolution was developing 'spontaneously.' The S.D.'s still put the problem of 'unleashing' the revolution before the problem of its 'organization.' Under such conditions, the traditional influence of the Populists had still not been forced out by S.D. agitation, and among the peasantry, populist influence was unquestionably predominant. There was still the possibility of instilling more moderate 'bourgeois' political tendencies in the masses. This was confirmed even by the jealousy of the S.D.'s toward potential competition from the 'Zemstvoists,' as they indiscriminately labeled their opponents at that time. The genuine Zemstvo Constitutionalists specifically included in their political calculations the possibility of propaganda among the masses. It was precisely this last group that came more and more into its own as the political currents separated. With all the defections to the right, its composition still remained, rather indefinitely, on the left. This must be judged in the context of a general displacement of the political struggle in that direction. It must not be forgotten that we were concerned with the creation, not of a revolutionary party, but of a constitutional one, whose task would be to carry on the struggle with parliamentary means. In the spectrum of political parties which had sprung up, the parliamentary place had yet to be filled, and it was up to us to fill it. Unless it was filled, it would have been impossible even to think of establishing a constitutional regime in Russia. To place this special task before the future party became more and more my personal task, and my activities among those elements which displayed a tendency to join our future party were increasingly devoted to it.

The immediate issue to be decided was, then, the question of participation or nonparticipation in the elections to the 'Bulygin' Duma [A.G.

Bulygin was appointed Minister of the Interior in January 1905], which served as a touchstone for choosing one road or the other – revolution or constitution. We saw that, on this question, vacillation persisted even in the leftist groups ... From the superficial view of the congress, and from the outcome of the clash there with police carrying out the will of the ministry, one could see at once how much the political situation had changed during the interval between May and July. This time we met in the tremendous home of Prince Pavel Dmitrievich Dolgorukov, in the neglected garden on Znamensky Lane, the same house where the host's late elder brother, Nikolai, and myself had once studied for the gymnasium exams. Someone no doubt still remembers the photograph of the numerous (235) members of this congress in the foreground of the princely palace. Assistant Minister [A.F.] Trepov declared beforehand that the decisions of the congress would be illegal. To the police who came to disperse the congress, the presidium simply referred to the 'tsar's will'; that is, to convey the promise of the Tsar 'to all friends living on the land and in the cities.' The Bureau of the Congresses carefully prepared the work of the congress, and in place of the Bulygin project, which the congress had rejected, it offered its own project of 'a fundamental law,' which had been published on the opening day of the congress in Russkie Vedomosti. The bureau's project was adopted 'on the first reading.' V.D. Nobokov then proposed 'to defend the natural rights,' as stated in the resolutions of the November Congress of 1904, 'by all peaceful means, not excluding disobedience of the orders of the authorities which violate these rights.' In accordance with a proposal of the brothers Pavel and Peter Dolgorukov, it was decided 'to maintain the closest contact with the broad masses' in order to 'evaluate the impending reforms together with the people,' 'to win the freedom necessary to carry out the reforms,' and 'to work out at the local level the problems of putting into practice the electoral system devised by the general Zemstvo Congress.' The extremely daring formulation of these barely masked resolutions can be properly appreciated when one remembers that they implied the introduction of a Constitutional Assembly and universal elections virtually without the permission of the authorities. The congress adopted the text of the address to the people which the bureau prepared, but it showed itself extremely cautious when the question arose as to distributing this appeal among the masses. Several speakers considered the address to the people as much 'too revolutionary a means.' When the discussions came around to the main specific task – the elections to the Bulygin Duma – the congress, after stormy debates, displayed still more caution and left the question open. The scope of the congress was thus defined, from the adoption of semirevolutionary principles to a realistic political movement, given the prevailing circumstances.

For a unified party, this scope was too broad. Still, the attitudes of the future members were clarified, if not the extent of their preparedness. But the work on the political unification of the party had only begun.

Paul Milyukov, *Political Memoires* 1905–1917, Ann Arbor: University of Michigan Press, 1967, pp. 35–6.

DOCUMENT 3   KERENSKY'S DESCRIPTION OF THE
MARCH REVOLUTION

As one of the chief actors in the Russian Provisional Government, Aleksandr Kerensky tries here to debunk the Bolshevik view of the events of 1917, and particularly the role of the Soviet. While the account presented here is more emotional than objective, there is some justification for Kerensky's portrait of cooperation between the government and the Soviet in the months after the revolution.

The peculiarities of the social structure of Russia had always clearly indicated that in the event of a revolution or the introduction of universal suffrage, the principal role in Russian politics would pass to the parties which had the support of the working class and the toiling masses. And this was exactly what did occur. On the very first day after the suicide of tsarism, it was not only the Russia of the nobility that was swept away, but even the liberal-capitalist Russia became a mere shadow of its former self. Our tragedy lay in the fact that at the time of this unprecedented social upheaval, its essential nature was not understood, not felt, either by the leaders of the middle class in the Duma or by those of the proletariat in the newly formed Soviet.

The majority of the 'temporary committee of the Duma' were members of the Progressive bloc. Apart from a project of government policy drafted as far back as 1915, the bloc had also an outline proposal of political changes in the event of a coup d'état and a regency. There was even a preliminary list of ministers against this contingency. It is quite natural and logical, therefore, that at first the temporary committee, deeming itself to be at the head of the revolution, never doubted that the time had come to put the plans of the Progressive bloc into practice. In the afternoon of March 12 the journalists asked the liberal leader of the bloc, what would be the program of the new government to be organized by the Duma? Professor Miliukov, a clever historian though never a statesman, answered promptly and decisively: 'Needless to say the government program will be that of the

Progressive bloc.' I stood by and could not believe my ears, thinking he was joking. But he was tragically in earnest. He had no doubt that the destinies of Russia were henceforth firmly in the hands of the liberals and their more conservative political allies. Under a regency the cabinet would have been composed of members of the bloc with a slight bias to the right. Now the bias would have to be just a little to the left: a few more Kadets, that is all!

Even by daybreak on March 13, however, it was clear that such a government was a forlorn hope: in the course of a day and a night the relative strength of the radical and socialist parties had increased incredibly. At a conference of the leaders of the Progressive bloc it was decided to offer two seats in the proposed government to members of the Soviet. The portfolio of labor to Chkheidze, the chairman; justice – to me, the vice-chairman …

It is generally imagined, both in Russia and outside, that immediately after March 12 there began a struggle for power between the Provisional Government and the soviets. This is fiction pure and simple! From the first day of their existence until Lenin's coup in November, the soviets made no claims whatsoever to government power. Their leaders – excepting the Bolsheviks, of course – quite honestly accepted the Provisional Government as the only central national authority, and they tried to support this authority in every way. Even in April, 1917, when the relations between the Provisional Government and the Petrograd Soviet were particularly strained, one of the recognized directors of soviet policy, the Social Democrat, Dan [F.I. Dan, a Menshevik leader], declared in no uncertain terms: 'We want it made absolutely clear and definite that it is a libel to say that the Soviet of the Workers' and Soldiers' Deputies wishes to take part in the administration. We want to have it understood: The ruler is the Provisional Government.' In practice the soviets were admittedly a very questionable support for the government; but this was not because their leaders wanted to seize power; it was simply that with their ingrained habit of fighting the autocracy they often unconsciously used the same subversive methods against their own revolutionary leaders. Thus they often failed to act with a proper sense of responsibility.

Still, all the friction between the government and the soviets notwithstanding, the latter had fulfilled a tremendously important function during the early days of the revolution and, contrary to the opinion very often expressed, quite a positive, useful function. This function is generally little understood even to this day. Some confuse the soviets that actually existed with the myth invented by Bolshevik demagogues. Others lay the responsibility for all the inevitable destructive consequences of tsarism's suicide at the door of the soviets' alleged disruptive agitation. As a matter of fact, the soviets never were either 'a new revolutionary state-form' or an instrument for the destruction of the state. On the contrary. At the worst moment of disintegration at the time of the greatest anarchy, during the first days of the revolution, the soviets were very effective in organizing the diffused, scattered masses and in re-establishing the rudiments of discipline.

However, it would be difficult to understand the part the soviets had to play without reference to the condition of Russia immediately following the collapse of the monarchy. The old government disappeared on the morning of March 12; the new did not appear until the morning of March 15. Three days without any government whatsoever. An empire with an army of over 10 million men fighting at the front, and in the throes of a great economic crisis, suddenly left, as it were, at the mercy of the winds. It is true that, except for Petrograd itself, the army and the whole country accepted the revolution without any resistance, quite peacefully and joyfully. There had been excesses against the imaginary, more often than the real, partisans of the old regime, but there was no resistance whatsoever to the new. On the contrary, the entire administrative machine disappeared with incredible rapidity together with the monarchy. Those who did not witness the early days of the Russian revolution from its storm center cannot imagine the extent of the collapse of the administrative structure: it was a veritable catastrophe! The people hated the fallen regime so much that they had come to regard the state itself as at least an alien if not actually a hostile institution. The tsar, the ministers, the governors, the urban and rural police – everything had disappeared within three days of Rodzianko's receiving the Ukase of Prorogation. On March 12 there flared up a ferocious mutiny of the soldiers against the officers in Kronstadt. Similar horrors were brewing in Helsingfors, the chief base of our Baltic Grand Fleet. At the front, in the army, the traditional relations between the officers and men broke down immediately upon the receipt of news of the revolution and the fall of the monarchy. Discipline, civic and military, disappeared throughout the land. No one was prepared to obey any longer; those who were used to command no longer knew how, or did not dare. Even the zemstvos, which had been the true pride of progressive Russia, had lost their former prestige in the eyes of the peasants; after all, they had been elected on a property qualification basis, they were gentry-ridden!

What was to be done? How was the country to be governed in the midst of a great war without any means of administrative compulsion, with the towns choked with thousands and thousands of recruits? What if at this moment of chaos and anarchy the workmen, the peasants, the soldiers, and every national minority were to remember the bitter injustice, insults, and torments that they had suffered under the tsar? What if the city rabble was to begin decorating the lampposts with their masters and owners of the day before – nobles, officials, generals – every one who had a 'starched collar and a tie'?...

But nothing like that occurred. What happened I can only describe as a miracle. Amidst the chaos and darkness of the collapse of tsarism, there rose the bright sun of liberty to shine on a country broken with suffering. And somehow the feeling of hatred and vengeance melted, and disappeared from the human heart! Turning back now to those terrifying first weeks of the revolution, I am surprised, not that innocent blood was shed, but that there was so little of it; that is what strikes me most now. Today, when the gross reaction of Bolshevik and Hitlerite dictatorship, steeped in hatred and human blood, is blasphemously called revolution, it seems a downright insult to apply the same name to that time of unselfish idealism and boundless enthusiasm, that time of the splendid impulse towards truth, liberty and social justice, which we knew in Russia in the spring of 1917!

Aleksandr Kerensky, *The Crucifixion of Liberty*, trans. G. Kerensky from the unpublished Russian manuscript, New York: John Day, 1934, pp. 37–8.

DOCUMENT 4   THE ACT OF ABDICATION OF TSAR NIKOLAY II

Nikolay II resigned quietly and with some dignity, though for some time he had seemed unaware of the real state of affairs in Petrograd. Initially he resigned in favour of his son Aleksey, but later this was retracted and in the document below he passes the monarchy on to his younger brother, Mikhail Aleksandrovich, a man who had spent much of his early career pursuing a woman who was divorced and separated from her second husband [27]. Wisely, Mikhail declined to take the throne.

In days of great struggle with the foreign enemy, who for almost three years has endeavored to enslave our motherland, it has pleased the Lord God to send to Russia a new heavy trial.

The internal popular disturbances that have begun threaten to be reflected disastrously in the further conduct of the stubborn war.

The fate of Russia, the honor of our heroic army, the welfare of the people, all the future of our dear fatherland demand the prosecution of the war to a victorious end at any cost.

The ruthless enemy is straining his last forces, and the hour is already near when our valiant army, together with our glorious allies, can finally break the enemy. In these decisive days in the life of Russia we have found it a conscientious duty to help our people to close unity and the gathering of all their forces for the speediest achievement of victory and, in agreement with the State Duma, We have recognized it as good to renounce the throne of the Russian state and to lay down the supreme power.

Not desiring to part with Our beloved son, We transfer Our Succession to Our brother the Grand Duke Michael Alexandrovitch, and We bless him upon his accession to the throne of the Russian state.

We enjoin upon Our brother to direct affairs of state in full and inviolable union with the representatives of the people in the legislative assemblies on the bases which will be established by them, pledging in this an inviolable oath in the name of the warmly beloved motherland.

We summon all faithful sons of the fatherland to fulfill their sacred duty to it by obeying the Tsar in the difficult moment of general trial and to help him, along with the representatives of the people, to bring the Russian state out on the road of victory, prosperity and glory. May the Lord God help Russia.

Pskov, March 2 (15), 1917.

William Henry Chamberlin, *The Russian Revolution* 1817–1921, 2 vols, New York: Macmillan, 1957, Vol. 1, pp. 430–1.

DOCUMENT 5   THE APRIL THESES

Lenin's April Theses were to change the course of Bolshevik policy drastically following the success of the March Revolution. They maintained that the policy of cooperation with other socialist parties to maintain the Provisional Government in power was to be ended, and support given to a takeover by the soviets. Though the strategy was to work in the long term, the theses were quietly shelved in July, as a majority in the Petrograd Soviet, composed of SRs and Mensheviks, rejected a policy of seeking power and, on the contrary, made up the majority of the Cabinet of the Provisional Government.

1. In our attitude toward the War, which on Russia's side, also under the new Government of Lvov and Co. remains a predatory imperialistic war as a result of the capitalist character of this Government, not the least concessions to 'revolutionary defensivism' are permissible.

The classconscious proletariat can give its consent to revolutionary war, which would really justify revolutionary defensivism, only on these conditions: (a) The passing of power into the hands of the proletariat and of those poorest groups of the peasantry who side with it; (b) Renunciation of all annexations in deeds, and not in words; (c) Complete breach with all the interests of capital.

In view of the unquestionable sincerity of the masses of the advocates of revolutionary defensivism, who recognize the War as a matter of necessity and not for the sake of conquests, in view of the fact that they are deceived by the bourgeoisie, we must especially fully, insistently, patiently explain to them their mistake, explain the inseparable connection of capital with imperialistic war, prove that without the overthrow of capital it is impossible to end the War with a truly democratic and not an annexationist peace.

Organization of the most widespread propaganda for this viewpoint in the Army in the field.

Fraternization.

2. The peculiarity of the present period in Russia is the transition from the first stage of the Revolution, which gave power to the bourgeoisie as a result of the insufficient classconsciousness and organization of the proletariat, to its second stage, which must give power into the hands of the proletariat and the poorest classes of the peasantry.

This transition is characterized, on the one hand, by the maximum of legal toleration (Russia *now* is the freest of all the belligerent countries in the world), on the other hand, by the absence of violence against the masses and, finally, by the ignorantly trustful attitude of the masses toward the Government of the capitalists, the worst enemies of peace and socialism.

This peculiarity demands from us the ability to adjust ourselves to the *special* conditions of Party work in the midst of unprecedentedly numerous masses of the proletariat who are just awakening to political life.

3. No support to the Provisional Government, explanation of the complete falsity of all its promises, especially regarding the renunciation of annexations. Exposure, not the impermissible, illusion-breeding 'demand,' that this Government, a Government of capitalists, should cease to be imperialistic.

4. Recognition of the fact that in the majority of Soviets of Workers' Deputies our Party is in the minority, and so far in a weak minority, against the block of all the petty-bourgeois opportunist N.S.S.R. [People's Socialists and Socialist Revolutionaries] elements, which succumb to the influence of the bourgeoisie and carry out its influence on the proletariat, including the OK [a Menshevik organization] (Chkheidze, Tseretelli and others), Steklov, etc.

Explanation to the masses that the Soviet of Workers' Deputies is the sole possible form of revolutionary government, and that, therefore, our problem, so long as this Government submits to the influence of the bourgeoisie, can only be patient, systematic, insistent explanation of mistakes and tactics, adapted especially to the practical needs of the masses.

While we are in the minority we carry on the work of criticism and explanation of mistakes, at the same time advocating the necessity that all state power should pass into the hands of Soviets of Workers' Deputies, so that the masses by experience should free themselves from mistakes.

5. Not a parliamentary republic – the return to this from the Soviet of Workers', Farmhands' and Peasants' Deputies in the whole country, from below to above.

Elimination of the police, army and bureaucracy (i.e., replacement of the regular army by a general arming of the people).

Pay to all officials, who are to be elected and removed at any time, not more than the pay of a good worker.

6. In the agrarian programme the emphasis is to be placed on the Soviets of Farmhands' Deputies.

Confiscation of all land belonging to landlords.

Nationalization of all land in the country, management of the land by local Soviets of Farmhands' and Peasants' Deputies. Selection of Soviets of deputies from the poorest peasants. Creation out of every big estate (between 100 and 300 desyatinas in size) of a model farm under the control of farmhands' deputies and at public expense.

7. Immediate fusion of all the banks of the country into one general national bank and the introduction of control of the Soviet of Workers' Deputies over this bank.

8. Not the 'introduction' of socialism as our *immediate* task, but the transition only to control of the Soviet of Workers' Deputies over public production and distribution of products.

9. Party problems:

(a) Immediate convocation of a Party Congress.

(b) Change of the Party programme, mainly as follows:

   1. About imperialism and the imperialistic War.

   2. About the attitude to the state and *our* demand for a 'state commune' (i.e., a state modelled on the Paris Commune).

   3. Correction of the out-of-date minimum programme.

(c) Change of the name of the Party.

10. Revival of the International.

Initiative for the creation of a revolutionary International, an International against the social-chauvinists and against 'the Centre.'

N. Lenin

William Henry Chamberlin, *The Russian Revolution, 1817–1921*, 2 vols, New York: Macmillan, 1957, Vol. 1, pp. 441–3.

DOCUMENT 6   **KORNILOV'S APPEAL TO THE RUSSIAN PEOPLE**

Kornilov's uprising in September 1917 was the only attempt from the Far Right to mount a threat to the Provisional Government. It was primarily an attack on the Bolsheviks and their alleged collaboration with the Germans, an accusation given some weight by the German role in Lenin's return to Petrograd in April 1917. Kornilov had recently been appointed Commander-in-Chief of the Russian army by Kerensky, and there has been considerable speculation that the latter may have given Kornilov the impression, accidentally or otherwise, that he should concentrate power in his own hands.

Russian People.

Our great Motherland is perishing.

The final hour is near.

Compelled to come out openly, I, General Kornilov, declare that the Provisional Government under the pressure of the Bolshevik majority of the Soviets, acts in full agreement with the plans of the German General Staff, simultaneously with the impending descent of hostile forces on the Riga coast, destroys the Army and upsets the country from within. The painful consciousness of the inevitable destruction of the country commands me at this threatening moment to summon all Russian people to save the perishing motherland. Let all in whose breasts beat Russian hearts, all who believe in God and His churches pray to the Lord God for the greatest miracle: the salvation of our native land. I, General Kornilov, the son of a Cossack peasant, declare to all that personally I want nothing except the preservation of Great Russia, and I vow to bring the people, through victory over the enemy, to the Constituent Assembly, at which the people will itself decide its own fate and choose its own form of government. I cannot betray Russia into the hands of its historic enemy, the German tribe, and make the Russian people slaves of the Germans.

Kornilov

9 September 1917

> William Henry Chamberlin, *The Russian Revolution, 1817–1921*, 2 vols, New York: Macmillan, 1957, Vol. 1, p. 462.

DOCUMENT 7   **THE FINAL DAYS OF THE PROVISIONAL GOVERNMENT**

John Reed (1887–1920) was an American poet and revolutionary who befriended Lenin and provided an absorbing eyewitness account of the revolution. Subsequently he was one of the founders of the Communist Party of the United States.

September and October are the worst months of the Russian year – especially the Petrograd year. Under dull grey skies, in the shortening days, the rain fell drenching, incessant. The mud underfoot was deep, slippery and clinging, tracked everywhere by heavy boots, and worse than usual because of the complete break-down of the Municipal administration. Bitter damp winds rushed in from the Gulf of Finland, and the chill fog rolled through the streets. At night, for motives of economy as well as fear of Zeppelins, the street-lights were few and far between; in private dwellings and apartment-houses the electricity was turned on from six o'clock until midnight, with candles forty cents apiece and little kerosene to be had. It was dark from three in the afternoon to ten in the morning. Robberies and housebreakings increased. In apartment houses the men took turns at all-night guard duty, armed with loaded rifles. This was under the Provisional Government.

Week by week food became scarcer. The daily allowance of bread fell from a pound and a half to a pound, then three quarters, half, and a quarter pound. Toward the end there was a week without any bread at all. Sugar one was entitled to at the rate of two pounds a month – if one could get it at all, which was seldom. A bar of chocolate or a pound of tasteless candy cost anywhere from seven to ten rubles – at least a dollar. There was milk for about half the babies in the city; most hotels and private houses never saw it for months. In the fruit season apples and pears sold for a little less than a ruble a piece on the street-corner ...

For milk and bread and sugar and tobacco one had to stand in a queue long hours in the chill rain. Coming home from an all-night meeting I have seen the kvost (tail) beginning to form before dawn, mostly women, some with babies in their arms ... Carlyle, in his French Revolution, has described the French people as distinguished above all others by their faculty of standing in queue. Russia had accustomed herself to the practice, begun in the reign of Nikolay the Blessed as long ago as 1915, and from then continued to intermittently until the summer of 1917, when it settled down as the regular order of things. Think of the poorly-clad people standing on the iron-white streets of Petrograd whole days in the Russian winter! I have listened in the bread-lines, hearing the bitter, acrid note of discontent which from time to time burst up through the miraculous good nature of the Russian crowd ...

Of course all the theatres were going every night, including Sundays. Karsavina appeared in a new Ballet at the Marinsky, all dance-loving Russia coming to see her. Shaliapin was singing. At the Alexandrinsky they were reciting Meyerhold's production of Tolstoy's 'Death of Ivan the Terrible'; and at that performance I remember noticing a student of the Imperial School of Pages, in his dress uniform, who stood up correctly between the acts and faced the empty Imperial box, with its eagles all erased ... The Krivoye Zerkalo staged a sumptuous version of Schnitzler's 'Reigen.'

Although the Hermitage and other picture galleries had been evacuated to Moscow, there were weekly exhibitions of paintings. Hordes of the female intelligentzia went to hear lectures on Art, Literature, and the Easy Philosophies. It was a particularly active season for Theosophists. And the Salvation Army, admitted to Russia for the first time in history, plastered the walls with announcements of gospel meetings, which amused and astounded Russian audiences ...

As in all such times, the petty conventional life of the city went on, ignoring the Revolution as much as possible. The poets made verses – but not about the Revolution. The realistic painters painted scenes from mediaeval Russian history – anything but the Revolution. Young ladies from the provinces came up to the capital to learn French and cultivate their voices, and the gay young beautiful officers wore their gold-trimmed crimson bashliki and their elaborate Caucasian swords around the hotel lobbies. The ladies of the minor bureaucratic set took tea with each other in the afternoon, carrying each her little gold or silver or jeweled sugar-box, and half a loaf of bread in her muff, and wished that the Tsar were back, or that the Germans would come, or anything that would solve the servant problem ... The daughter of a friend of mine came home one afternoon in hysterics because the woman street-car conductor had called her 'Comrade!'

John Reed, *Ten Days That Shook the World*, New York: Boni and Liveright, 1919, pp. 11–13.

DOCUMENT 8   **LENIN DEMANDS THAT THE BOLSHEVIKS TAKE POWER**

Once the Bolsheviks had acquired a majority in the Petrograd and Moscow soviets, and having acquired weapons among their Red Guards as a result of the failed Kornilov putsch, Lenin was anxious that the opportunity to seize power through force should not be lost. The following is a portion of Lenin's letter to the Central Committee and the Petrograd and Moscow committees of the RSDWP [b].

The majority of the people are *on our side*. This was proved by the long and painful course of events from May 6 to August 31 and to September 12. The majority gained in the Soviets of the metropolitan cities *resulted* from the people coming over *to our side*. The wavering of the Socialist Revolutionaries and Mensheviks and the increase in the number of internationalists within their ranks prove the same thing ...

Why must the Bolsheviks assume power *at this very moment*?

Because the impending surrender of Petrograd will make our chances a hundred times less favourable.

And it is *not in our power* to prevent the surrender of Petrograd while the army is headed by Kerensky and Co.

Nor can we 'wait' for the Constituent Assembly, for by surrendering Petrograd Kerensky and Co. *can* always *frustrate* its convocation. Our Party alone, on taking power, can secure the Constituent Assembly's convocation; it will then accuse the other parties of procrastination and will be able to substantiate its accusations ...

The point is to make the *task* clear to the Party. The present task must be an *armed uprising* in Petrograd and Moscow (with its region), the seizing of power and the overthrow of the government ...

History will not forgive us if we do not assume power now ...

V.I. Lenin, *Selected Works in Three Volumes*, Moscow: Progress Publishers, 1973,
Vol. 2, pp. 362–3.

DOCUMENT 9	THE MENSHEVIKS AND SOCIAL REVOLUTIONARIES PROTEST AGAINST THE BOLSHEVIK UPRISING

At the Second All-Russian Congress of the Soviets the Mensheviks and SRs protested against the Bolshevik uprising, which seemed to them a blatant power grab that was opposed fundamentally to Marxist teaching. Following the protest, the two groups walked out of the Congress.

Taking into consideration

1. That a military conspiracy was carried out and achieved by the Bolshevik Party in the name of the Soviet behind the backs of all the other parties and fractions, represented in the Soviets;

2. That the seizure of power by the Petrograd Soviet on the eve of the Congress of Soviets amounts to disorganization and break-up of the whole Soviet organization and undermines the significance of the Congress as the authorized representative of the revolutionary democracy;

3. That this conspiracy throws the country into civil strife, thwarts the Constituent Assembly, creates a threat of military catastrophe and leads to the triumph of counterrevolution;

4. That the sole possible peaceful way out of the situation is to negotiate with the Provisional Government about the organization of a Government, based on all groups of the democracy;

5. That the Russian Social Democratic Labor Party (united) considers it an obligation to the working class not only to repudiate, for itself, any responsibility for the activities of the Bolsheviki, who hide behind the Soviet banner, but also to warn the workers and soldiers against a policy of adventures that is fatal to the country and the Revolution: –

The fraction of the Russian Social Democratic Labor Party (united) leaves the present Congress, inviting all other fractions, which, like itself, refuse to bear responsibility for the activities of the Bolsheviki, to meet immediately to consider the situation.

William Henry Chamberlin, *The Russian Revolution, 1817–1921*, 2 vols, New York: Macmillan, 1957, Vol. 1, p. 470.

DOCUMENT 10	THE DECREE ON PEACE

The Decree on Peace demonstrated that the Bolsheviks intended to adhere to their promises of 1917. It also resonates with official optimism, personified by Lenin and Trotsky, that a world workers' revolution was at hand after three painful years of war. Like Marx, Lenin considered that a

socialist revolution was most likely to break out in the advanced nations of
Europe: France, Britain and Germany.

The workers' and peasants' government, created by the Revolution of
October 24–25 and basing itself on the Soviets of Workers', Soldiers' and
Peasants' Deputies, calls upon all the belligerent peoples and their govern-
ments to start immediate negotiations for a just, democratic peace.

By a just or democratic peace, for which the overwhelming majority of
the working class and other working people of all the belligerent countries,
exhausted, tormented and racked by the war, are craving – a peace that has
been most definitely and insistently demanded by the Russian workers and
peasants ever since the overthrow of the tsarist monarchy – by such a peace
the government means an immediate peace without annexations (i.e.,
without the seizure of foreign lands, without the forcible incorporation of
foreign nations) and without indemnities.

The Government of Russia proposes that this kind of peace be immediately concluded by all the belligerent nations, and expresses its readiness to
take all the resolute measures now, without the least delay, pending the final
ratification of all the terms of such a peace by authoritative assemblies of
the people's representatives of all countries and all nations.

In accordance with the sense of justice of democrats in general, and of
the working classes in particular, the government conceives the annexation
or seizure of foreign lands to mean every incorporation of a small or weak
nation into a large or powerful state without the precisely, clearly and voluntarily expressed consent and wish of that nation, irrespective of the time
when such forcible incorporation took place, irrespective also of the degree
of development or backwardness of the nation forcibly annexed to the
given state, or forcibly retained within its borders, and irrespective, finally,
of whether this nation is in Europe or in distant, overseas countries.

If any nation whatsoever is forcibly retained within the borders of a given
state, if, in spite of its expressed desire – no matter whether expressed in the
press, at public meetings, in the decisions of parties, or in protests and uprisings against national oppressions of parties – it is not accorded the right
to decide the forms of its state existence by a free vote, taken after the
complete evacuation of the troops of the incorporating or, generally,
of the stronger nation and without the least pressure being brought to bear,
such incorporation is annexation, i.e., seizure and violence.

The government considers it the greatest of crimes against humanity to
continue this war over the issue of how to divide among the strong and rich
nations the weak nationalities they have conquered, and solemnly announces
its determination immediately to sign terms of peace to stop this war on

the terms indicated, which are equally just for all nationalities without exception.

At the same time the government declares that it does not regard the above-mentioned peace terms as an ultimatum; in other words, it is prepared to consider any other peace terms, and insists only that they be advanced by any of the belligerent countries as speedily as possible, and that in the peace proposals there should be absolute clarity and the complete absence of all ambiguity and secrecy.

The government abolishes secret diplomacy, and, for its part, announces its firm intention to conduct all negotiations quite openly in full view of the whole people. It will proceed immediately with the full publication of the secret treaties endorsed or concluded by the government of landowners and capitalists from February to October 25, 1917. The government proclaims the unconditional and immediate annulment of everything contained in these secret treaties insofar as it is aimed, as is mostly the case, at securing advantages and privileges for the Russian landowners and capitalists and at the retention, or extension, of the annexations made by the Great Russians.

Proposing to the governments and peoples of all countries immediately to begin open negotiations for peace, the government, for its part, expresses its readiness to conduct these negotiations in writing, by telegraph, and by negotiations between representatives of the various countries, or at a conference of such representatives. In order to facilitate such negotiations, the government is appointing its plenipotentiary representative to neutral countries.

The government proposes an immediate armistice to the governments and peoples of all the belligerent countries, and, for its part, considers it desirable that this armistice should be concluded for a period of not less than three months, i.e., a period long enough to permit the completion of negotiations for peace with the participation of the representatives of all peoples or nations, without exception, involved in or compelled to take part in the war, and the summoning of authoritative assemblies of the representatives of the people of all countries for the final ratification of the peace terms.

While addressing this proposal for peace to the governments and peoples of all the belligerent countries, the Provisional Workers' and Peasants' Government of Russia appeals in particular also to the class-conscious workers of the three most advanced nations of mankind and the largest states participating in the present war, namely, Great Britain, France and Germany. The workers of these countries have made the greatest contributions to the cause of progress and socialism; they have furnished the great examples of the Chartist movement in England, a number of revolutions of historic importance effected by the French proletariat, and, finally, the heroic struggle against the Anti-Socialist Law in Germany and, the prolonged, persistent and disciplined work of creating mass proletarian organisations in Germany, a work which serves as a model to the workers of the whole world. All these examples of proletarian heroism and historical creative work are a pledge that the workers of the countries mentioned will understand the duty that now faces them of saving mankind from the horrors of war and its consequences, that these workers, by comprehensive, determined, and supremely vigorous action, will help us to conclude peace successfully, and at the same time emancipate the labouring and exploited masses of our population from all forms of slavery and all forms of exploitation.

The workers' and peasants' government, created by the Revolution of October 24–25 and basing itself on the support of the Soviets of Workers', Soldiers' and Peasants' Deputies, must start immediate negotiations for peace. Our appeal must be addressed both to the governments and to the peoples. We cannot ignore the governments, for that would delay the possibility of concluding peace, and the people's government dare not do that; but we have no right not to appeal to the peoples at the same time. Everywhere there are differences between the governments and the peoples, and we must therefore help the peoples to intervene in questions of war and peace. We will, of course, insist upon the whole of our programme for a peace without annexations and indemnities. We shall not retreat from it; but we must not give our enemies an opportunity to say that their conditions are different from ours and that therefore it is useless to start negotiations with us. No, we must deprive them of that advantageous position and not present our terms in the form of an ultimatum. Therefore the point is included that we are willing to consider any peace terms and all proposals. We shall consider them, but that does not necessarily mean that we shall accept them. We shall submit them for consideration to the Constituent Assembly which will have the power to decide what concessions can and what cannot be made. We are combating the deception practised by governments which pay lip-service to peace and justice, but in fact wage annexationist and predatory wars. No government will say all it thinks. We, however, are opposed to secret diplomacy and will act openly in full view of the whole people. We do not close our eyes to difficulties and never have done. War cannot be ended by refusal, it cannot be ended by one side. We are proposing an armistice for three months, but shall not reject a shorter period, so that the exhausted army may breathe freely, even if only for a little while; moreover, in all the civilised countries national assemblies must be summoned for the discussion of the terms.

In proposing an immediate armistice, we appeal to the class-conscious workers of the countries that have done so much for the development of the proletarian movement. We appeal to the workers of Britain, where there was the Chartist movement, to the workers of France, who have in repeated uprisings displayed the strength of their class-consciousness, and to the workers of Germany, who waged the fight against the Anti-Socialist Law and have created powerful organisations.

In the Manifesto of March 14, we called for the overthrow of the bankers, but, far from overthrowing our own bankers, we entered into an alliance with them. Now we have overthrown the government of the bankers.

The governments and the bourgeoisie will make every effort to unite their forces and drown the workers' and peasants' revolution in blood. But the three years of war have been a good lesson to the masses – the Soviet movement in other countries and the mutiny in the German navy, which was crushed by the officer cadets of Wilhelm the hangman [Kaiser Wilhelm II]. Finally, we must remember that we are not living in the depths of Africa, but in Europe, where news can spread quickly.

The workers' movement will triumph and will pave the way to peace and socialism. (*Prolonged applause.*)

[8 November 1917]

V.I. Lenin, *Selected Works in Three Volumes*, Moscow: Progress Publishers, 1973, Vol. 2, pp. 459–63.

DOCUMENT 11   THE DECREE ON LAND

The Decree on Land lambasts the Provisional Government for its failure to attend to the land question. In reality, much of the following decree was superfluous in that many of the measures stipulated had already been carried out by the peasants independently. In addition, a final settlement is left for the Constituent Assembly, a policy that the Provisional Government also followed. However, the decree is significant in that it embraces the second great promise of Bolshevik slogans: land (following peace).

We maintain that the revolution has proved and demonstrated how important it is that the land question should be put clearly. The outbreak of the armed uprising, the second, October, Revolution, clearly proves that the land must be turned over to the peasants. The government that has been overthrown and the compromising parties of the Mensheviks and the Socialist-Revolutionaries committed a crime when they kept postponing the settlement of the land question on various pretexts and thereby brought the country to economic chaos and a peasant revolt. Their talk about riots and anarchy in the countryside sounds false, cowardly, and deceitful. Where and when have riots and anarchy been provoked by wise measures? If the government had acted wisely, and if their measures had met the needs of the poor peasants would there have been unrest among the peasant masses? But all the measures of the government, approved by the Avksentyev and Dan Soviets, went counter to the interests of the peasants and compelled them to revolt.

Having provoked the revolt, the government raised a hue and cry about the riots and anarchy, for which they themselves were responsible. They were going to crush it by blood and iron, but were themselves swept away by the armed uprising of the revolutionary soldiers, sailors and workers. The first duty of the government of the workers' and peasants' revolution must be to settle the land question, which can pacify and satisfy the vast masses of poor peasants. I shall read to you the clauses of a decree your Soviet Government must issue. In one of the clauses of this decree is embodied the Mandate to the Land Committees, compiled on the basis of 242 mandates from local Soviets of Peasants' Deputies.

Decree on Land
1) Landed proprietorship is abolished forthwith without any compensation.
2) The landed estates, as also all crown, monastery, and church lands, with all their livestock, implements, buildings and everything pertaining thereto, shall be placed at the disposal of the volost land committees and the uyezd [district] Soviets of Peasants' Deputies pending the convocation of the Constituent Assembly.
3) All damage to confiscated property, which henceforth belongs to the whole people, is proclaimed a grave crime to be punished by the revolutionary courts. The uyezd Soviets of Peasants' Deputies shall take all necessary measures to assure the observance of the strictest order during the confiscation of the landed estates, to determine the size of estates, and the particular estates subject to confiscation, to draw up exact inventories of all property confiscated and to protect in the strictest revolutionary way all agricultural enterprises transferred to the people, with all buildings, implements, livestock, stocks of produce, etc ...

[8 November 1917]

V.I. Lenin, *Selected Works in Three Volumes*, Moscow: Progress Publishers, 1973, Vol. 2, pp. 467–8.

DOCUMENT 12   **THE FORMATION OF THE FIRST SOVIET GOVERNMENT**

The announcement of the first Soviet government was a misleading document. It appears to be of a temporary nature as the Bolsheviks were anticipating that they could present the Constituent Assembly with a fait accompli. Lenin was soon to maintain, in the face of majority opposition in the assembly, that the soviets actually constituted a higher form of democracy than the assembly. The government was notable mainly for the obscurity of almost all its members (the exceptions were Lenin and Trotsky).

The All-Russia Congress of Soviets of Workers', Soldiers' and Peasants' Deputies resolves:

To establish a provisional workers' and peasants' government, to be known as the Council of People's Commissars, to govern the country until the Constituent Assembly is convened. The management of individual branches of state activity is entrusted to commissions whose members shall ensure the fulfilment of the programme announced by the Congress, and shall work in close contact with mass organizations of men and women workers, sailors, soldiers, peasants and office employees. Governmental authority is vested in a collegium of the chairmen of those commissions, i.e., the Council of People's Commissars.

Control over the activities of the People's Commissars with the right to replace them is vested in the All-Russia Congress of Soviets of Workers', Peasants' and Soldiers' Deputies and its Central Executive Committee.

At the present time the Council of People's Commissars is constituted as follows:

Chairman of the Council – *Vladimir Ulyanov (Lenin)*;
People's Commissar of the Interior – *A.I. Rykov*;
Agriculture – *V.P Milyutin*;
Labour – *A.G. Shlyapnikov*;
Army and Navy Affairs – a committee consisting of: *V.A. Ovseyenko (Antonov), N.V. Krylenko and P.Y. Dybenko*;
Commerce and Industry – *V.P. Nogin*;
Education – *A.V. Lunacharsky*;
Finance – *I.I. Skvortsov (Stepanov)*;
Foreign Affairs – *L.D. Bronstein (Trotsky)*;
Justice – *G.I. Oppokov (Lomov)*;
Food – *I.A. Teodorovich*;
Posts and Telegraph – *N.P. Avilov (Glebov)*;
Chairman for Nationalities Affairs – *J.V. Jugashvili (Stalin)*.

The office of People's Commissar of Railways is temporarily vacant.

[8 November 1917]

V.I. Lenin, *Selected Works in Three Volumes*, Moscow: Progress Publishers, 1973, Vol. 2, pp. 471–2.

A decree that bore the hallmark of Lenin, the Bolsheviks' official adherence to self-determination for the people of Russia won them many supporters in the borderlands of the north, west and south. Later the issue was the subject of differences between the two signatories of this document.

Decree of the Sovnarkom, November 15, 1917.

The November revolution of the workers and peasants began under the common banner of emancipation.

The peasants are being emancipated from the power of the landlords, for the landlord no longer has any property right in the land – that right has been abolished. The soldiers and sailors are being emancipated from the power of autocratic generals, for henceforth generals will be elective and subject to recall. The workers are being emancipated from the whims and arbitrary will of the capitalists, for henceforth workers' control will be established over mills and factories. Everything living and viable is being emancipated from hateful shackles.

There remain now only the peoples of Russia who have suffered and are suffering under an arbitrary yoke. Their emancipation must be considered at once and their liberation effected with resoluteness and finality.

During the tsarist times the peoples of Russia were systematically incited against one another. The results of this policy are well known: massacres and pogroms on the one hand, slavery and bondage on the other.

There can be and there must be no return to this shameful policy of provocation. Henceforth it must be replaced by a policy of voluntary and honest co-operation between the peoples of Russia.

During the period of imperialism, after the March Revolution, when the government passed into the hands of Cadet bourgeoisie the unconcealed policy of instigation gave way to one of cowardly distrust of the peoples of Russia, of caviling and provocation camouflaged by verbal declarations about the 'freedom' and 'equality' of peoples. The results of this policy, too, are well known – the growth of national enmity, the impairment of mutual trust.

An end must be made to this unworthy policy of falsehood and distrust, of cavil and provocation. Henceforth it must be replaced by an open and honest policy leading to complete mutual confidence among the peoples of Russia.

Only as the result of such a confidence can an honest and lasting union of the peoples of Russia be formed.

Only as the result of such a union can the workers and peasants of the peoples of Russia be welded into a revolutionary force capable of resisting all [counter-revolutionary] attempts on the part of the imperialist-annexationist bourgeoisie.

The Congress of Soviets, in June of this year, proclaimed the right of the peoples of Russia to free self-determination.

The Second Congress of Soviets, in November of this year, reaffirmed this inalienable right of the peoples of Russia more decisively and definitely.

In compliance with the will of these Congresses, the Soviet of People's Commissars has resolved to adopt as the basis of its activity on the problem of nationalities in Russia the following principles:

1. Equality and sovereignty of the peoples of Russia.

2. The right to free self-determination of peoples even to the point of separating and forming independent states.

3. Abolition of each and every privilege or limitation based on nationality or religion.

4. Free development of national minorities and ethnographic groups inhabiting Russian territory.

All concrete measures appertaining to the above declaration are to be decreed immediately upon the formation of a special commission for nationalities.

Iosif Dzhugashvili (Stalin)
Commissar for Nationalities

V. Ulianov (Lenin)
President of Soviet of People's Commissars

James Bunyan and H.H. Fisher, eds, *The Bolshevik Revolution of 1917–1918: Documents and Materials*, Stanford: Stanford University Press, 1934, pp. 282–3.

DOCUMENT 14   **THE FOUNDATION OF THE CHEKA**

The Cheka was founded to preserve the revolution, but was to re-emerge in different forms throughout the period of Soviet rule. It was one of the key organizations of Bolshevik and Soviet rule and a symbol of the ruthlessness of the regime. Its creation came as a shock to those who had suffered at the hands of the tsarist secret police, the Okhrana. The Cheka, however, was more pervasive and arbitrary than its tsarist predecessor.

Establishment of the Extraordinary Commission to Fight Counter-Revolution, Decree of the Sovnarkom, December 20, 1917.

The Commission is to be named the All-Russian Extraordinary Commission and is to be attached to the Soviet of People's Commissars. [This commission] is to make war on counter-revolution and sabotage ...

The duties of the Commission will be:

1. To persecute and break up all acts of counter-revolution and sabotage all over Russia, no matter what their origin.

2. To bring before the Revolutionary Tribunal all counter-revolutionists and saboteurs and to work out a plan for fighting them.

3. To make preliminary investigation only – enough to break up [the counter-revolutionary act].

The Commission is to be divided into sections: (a) the information [section], (b) the organization section (in charge of organising the fight against counter-revolution all over Russia) with branches, and (c) the fighting section.

The Commission will be formed tomorrow ... The Commission is to watch the press, saboteurs, strikers, and all the Socialist-Revolutionists of the Right. Measures [to be taken against these counter-revolutionists are] confiscation, confinement, deprivation of [food] cards, publication of the names of the enemies of the people, etc.

James Bunyan and H.H. Fisher, eds, *The Bolshevik Revolution of 1917–1918: Documents and Materials*, Stanford: Stanford University Press, 1934, pp. 297–8.

DOCUMENT 15   THE EMPOWERMENT OF THE FOOD COMMISSARIAT

The decree of 9 May 1918 was a critical part of the policy known as War Communism, maintaining that a group of richer peasants was deliberately hoarding grain. This decree was to make it difficult for the peasantry to keep any grain other than the amount needed for mere subsistence. It was the first stage of an artificially created class war in the countryside. Matters had become especially critical since Ukraine, the traditional grain heartland of the former Russian Empire, had fallen under German occupation.

The ruinous breakdown in the country's food supply, the disastrous inheritance of four years of war, continues to spread and to become more aggravated. While the consuming provinces are starving, there are now, as formerly, large reserves of grain which has not even been milled, from the harvests of 1916 and 1917, in the producing provinces. This grain is in the hands of the kulaks and the rich, in the hands of the village bourgeoisie. Well fed and provided for, having accumulated immense sums of money during the years of war, the village bourgeoisie remains stubbornly deaf and indifferent to the cries of the starving workers and poor peasants, and does not bring grain to the collection points. It counts on forcing the Government to make new and further increases in grain prices and at the same time sells grain in its own places at fabulous prices to grain speculators and bagmen.

There must be an end of this stubbornness of the greedy village kulaks and rich. Experience with the food problem in preceding years has shown that the breakdown of fixed prices for grain and the abolition of the grain monopoly, while it would make it possible for a handful of our capitalists to feast, would place grain absolutely out of reach for millions of the workers and would condemn them to an unavoidable death from hunger. To the violence of the owners of the grain against the starving poor the answer must be: violence against the bourgeoisie. Not one pood of grain must remain in the hands of its holders, except for the amount required for the sowing of their fields and the feeding of their families until the new harvest.

And this must be carried out immediately, especially after the occupation of Ukraina by the Germans, when we are forced to satisfy ourselves with grain resources which scarcely suffice for seeding and cut down the food supply.

Having considered the situation which has arisen and taking account of the fact that only with the strictest account and even distribution of all bread resources will Russia get out of the food crisis the All-Russian Soviet Executive Committee decided:

1. Affirming the unalterable character of the grain monopoly and of the fixed prices and also the necessity for a merciless struggle with the grain speculators and bagmen, to force every owner of grain to declare for delivery within a week after the announcement of this decision in every township all the surplus above the amount required for the seeding of the fields and for personal use, according to the established scales, until the new harvest. The order of these declarations is determined by the Food Commissariat through the local food organizations.

2. To call on all the working and unpropertied peasants to unite immediately for a merciless war against the kulaks.

3. To declare all who possess surplus grain and do not take it to the delivery points and also those who dissipate the grain reserves in making home-brewed liquor enemies of the people. To hand them over to a revolutionary court, with the provision that those who are found guilty should be condemned to imprisonment for not less than ten years, and should be driven forever from their village community, all their property being confiscated. The makers of liquor should also be condemned to forced labor.

4. In the event that someone is discovered with surplus grain which was not declared for delivery, according to Paragraph 1, the grain is taken away from him without compensation and the value of the undeclared surplus, reckoned in fixed prices, is paid half to the person who points out the hidden surplus and half to the village community, after the grain has actually been brought to the delivery points. Reports of hidden surplus stocks are to be made to the local food organizations.

Then, taking into consideration the facts that the struggle with the food crisis demands the application of quick and decisive measures, that the most effective carrying out of these measures, in turn, demands the centralization of all orders relating to food in a single institution and that this institution is the Food Commissariat, the All-Russian Soviet Central Executive Committee decides to give the Food Commissariat the following powers, to make possible a more successful struggle against the food crisis:

1. To promulgate compulsory decisions on food which go beyond the usual limits of the competence of the Food Commissariat.

2. To repeal the decisions of local food organizations and other bodies and institutions which contradict the plans and the information of the Food Commissariat.

3. To demand from institutions and organizations of all departments the unconditional and immediate execution of the orders of the Food Commissariat on the food question.

4. To apply armed force in the event that resistance is shown to the taking away of grain or other food products.

5. To dissolve or reorganize the local food organizations if they oppose the orders of the Food Commissariat.

6. To dismiss, replace, bring to revolutionary trial, arrest all holders of posts, employees of all departments and public organizations if they interfere with the orders of the Food Commissariat in a disorganizing way.

7. To transmit these powers (with the exception of the right to arrest, Point 6) to other persons and local institutions, with the approval of the Council of People's Commissars.

8. All those measures of the Food Commissariat which, by their nature, are connected with the departments of railroad transportation and of the Supreme Economic Council are put into effect in contact with the corresponding departments.

9. The decisions and orders of the Food Commissariat, issued in virtue of the present full powers, are examined by the Collegium of the Food Commissariat, which has the right, without stopping the execution of the orders, to lodge complaints about them with the Council of People's Commissars.

The present decree comes into force from the day of its signature and is put into effect by telegraph.

President of the All-Russian Soviet Central Executive Committee, Y. Sverdlov,
President of the Council of People's Commissars, V. Ulianov (Lenin),
Secretary of the All-Russian Soviet Central Executive Committee, Avanesov.

William Henry Chamberlin, *The Russian Revolution*, 1817–1921, 2 vols, New York: Macmillan, 1957, Vol. 1, pp. 509–11.

The committees of the village poor were the means to create class strife in the countryside. The Bolsheviks perceived the poor peasants as their natural allies, who would join them in the struggle against the kulaks. The latter group was never clearly defined, and although Soviet sources always maintained that the rich peasants comprised a small minority of the rural population, much larger percentages were encompassed in anti-kulak campaigns.

Sverdlov, Y.A. 'Committees of the Village Poor,' Decree of the Central Executive Committee, June 11, 1918.

1. Volost and village committees of the poor, organized by local Soviets of Workers' and Peasants' Deputies with the participation of the (local) food departments and under the general control of the People's Commissariat of Food and the All-Russian Central Executive Committee, shall be established everywhere ...

2. Both native and newly arrived inhabitants of the village may elect and be elected to volost and village committees of the poor, with the exception of notorious kulaks ... who possess grain surpluses and other food products, and owners of commercial and industrial enterprises using hired labor, etc.

Note: Peasants employing labor on farms which do not exceed the consumption standard may elect and be elected to the committees of the poor.

3. The volost and village committees of the poor discharge the following duties:

a) Distribution of food, goods of prime necessity, and farming implements.

b) Assistance to local food departments in requisitioning surplus grain from kulaks and the rich ...

7. The distribution of grain, goods of prime necessity, and farming implements must accord with the standards set up by the gubernia food departments and conform to the general plans of the People's Commissariat of Food ...

8. For the time being and until the People's Commissar of Food makes special rulings, the basis of grain distribution shall be as follows:

a) Grain is distributed among the village poor in accordance with the established standards and free of charge, at the expense of the state. The distribution is made out of the grain surpluses which have been fully requisitioned from the kulaks and the rich in accordance with the decision of the gubernia and uezd soviets ... and have been delivered to the state grain storehouses ...

10. Volost committees of the poor are to take charge of the more complicated agricultural machinery and to organize communal cultivation of the fields and harvesting for the village poor; no charge will be made for the use of such machinery in places where the volost and village committees of the poor give energetic support to the food departments in requisitioning the surplus from the kulaks and the rich.

11. The Soviet of People's Commissars will place at the disposal of the People's Commissariat of Food such money as may be needed from time to time to execute this decree.

Y.A. Sverdlov
Chairman of the Executive Committee

V. Ulianov (Lenin)
President of the Sovnarkom

James Bunyan, ed., *Intervention, Civil War and Communism in Russia, April–December 1918: Documents and Materials*, Baltimore: Johns Hopkins University Press, 1936, pp. 472–3.

DOCUMENT 17   **HOW GRAIN REQUISITIONING WAS ORGANIZED**

Grain requisitions constituted a serious assault by the Bolshevik regime against the peasantry. It was maintained that the hoarding of grain constituted a serious threat to the urban centres, but the requisitions were both ruthless and arbitrary and often left the peasants without the means to support themselves. The policy lasted until March 1921.

1. Upon arriving at a village with his food detachment the political commissar shall call a meeting of the village poor and explain not only the meaning of the decree on organizing the lower classes of the village but also the role which the Russian counter-revolution and the kulaks are playing. He shall then ... organize a commitee to collect grain from the kulaks and distribute it ... among the needy peasants ...

2. The committee of the poor and the political commissar of the detachment shall then issue an order to the population to surrender all firearms. A part of the firearms is turned over to the newly elected committee in order to form an armed guard in connection with it; the rest must be sent by the commander of the detachment to the military commander of the gubernia. All machine guns and hand grenades must be confiscated....

3. Having done this the food agents, assisted by the detachment and the members of the commitee of the poor, shall proceed to make an inventory of all grain stores on hand ... as well as to uncover those that have been

hidden, with the exception of the grain, which ... the peasants need for their families, for seed, and for their cattle.

4. After the entire grain surplus of a given village has been ascertained, part of that surplus shall be distributed among the local poor ... and the rest shipped to the nearest government storage depot ...

7. Grain voluntarily surrendered in due time is to be paid for at a fixed price ... The grain of those failing to comply with the law ... shall be requisitioned at 25 percent less than the fixed price. Hidden grain is subject to confiscation ...

11. Those who violate the law of grain monopoly by selling grain to bagmen or wasting it for home-brew shall be arrested and given up to the gubernia Cheka.

12. The food-requisition detachment shall not leave a village until all grain surpluses have been delivered ...

A. Tsiurupa
People's Commissar of Food
20 August 1918

James Bunyan, ed., *Intervention, Civil War and Communism in Russia, April–December 1918: Documents and Materials*, Baltimore: Johns Hopkins University Press, 1936, pp. 478–9.

DOCUMENT 18   LENIN ON THE CIVIL WAR

For the Bolsheviks it was essential to point out that the alternative to their rule was the return of great landownership and capitalism, rather than a broader socialist coalition comprised of Mensheviks and Social Revolutionaries. This excerpt illustrates Lenin's superb propaganda techniques as he suggests that the landowners have not been defeated but have merely reverted to tactics of subterfuge.

Kolchak's victories in Siberia and the Urals have been a clear example to all of us that the least disorder, the slightest laxity or negligence at once serve to strengthen the landowners and the capitalists and make for their victory. For the landowners and capitalists have not been destroyed and do not consider themselves vanquished; every intelligent worker and peasant sees, knows, and realises that they have only been beaten and gone into hiding, are lying low, very often disguising themselves by a 'Soviet' 'protective' colouring. Many landowners have wormed their way into state farms and capitalists into various 'chief administrations' and 'central boards', acting the part of Soviet officials; they are watching every step of the Soviet government, waiting for it to make a mistake or show weakness, so as to overthrow it, to help the Czechoslovaks today and Denikin tomorrow ...

It is criminal to forget not only that the Kolchak movement began with trifles but also that the Mensheviks ... and S.R.s ... assisted its birth and directly supported it ... Since the Kolchak experience, can there still be peasants other than a few isolated individuals, who do not realize that a 'united front' with the Mensheviks and Social Revolutionaries means union with the abettors of Kolchak?

There is no middle course ... Either the dictatorship of the bourgeoisie ... or the dictatorship of the proletariat. He who has not learned this from the whole history of the nineteenth century is a hopeless idiot. And we in Russia have all seen how the Mensheviks and the Socialist-Revolutionaries dreamed of a middle course under Kerensky and under Kolchak ...

N. Lenin
August 24, 1919

> V.I. Lenin, *Selected Works in Three Volumes*, Moscow: Progress Publishers, 1973,
> Vol. 3, pp. 262–5.

DOCUMENT 19   TROTSKY'S VERSION OF THE KRONSTADT REVOLT

The Kronstadt Revolt proved a severe test for Trotsky as in part it demonstrated a lack of faith in his leadership over the army. This account is an attempt to rewrite the events to glorify the operations of the Red Army. In reality victory was attained after a series of embarrassing defeats and at a significant cost in casualties.

The Kronstadt events are a link in the steel chain that the imperialists of all countries are forging against Soviet power.

Under the slogan of minor improvements in the Soviet government, or of soviets without Communists, our native bourgeoisie and the international bourgeoisie wished to rally the workers and peasants against Soviet power.

The stock exchanges in Paris and Finland immediately made a correct estimation of the meaning of Kronstadt, and their loyal exponent Miliukov kept repeating: We must not frighten anyone, we must not oppose the soviets. We must use the slogan of nonparty soviets to destroy Soviet power.

A section of the sailors swallowed this bait. We waited as long as possible, for our blinded sailor comrades to see with their own eyes where the revolt was leading them. But we found ourselves faced with the danger that the ice would melt, and we were forced to strike a short, sharp and decisive blow.

With unparalleled heroism, by a feat of arms unprecedented in military history, our kursanti (military cadets) – and the Red Army units inspired by them – took a first-class naval fortress by storm.

Without firing a single shot these sons of worker-peasant Russia, true to the revolution, advanced across the ice, some perishing in silence but the rest still pressing on until final victory. They will never be forgotten by the toilers of Russia and the whole world. I believe that no stains will ever disfigure this banner. And at times of difficulty, if a weary doubt crosses your mind, remember Kronstadt and this banner, and go bravely forward to victory.

Pierre Frank, ed., *Kronstadt: By V.I. Lenin and Leon Trotsky*, New York: Monad Press, 1979, pp. 74–5.

DOCUMENT 20   **LENIN ADDRESSES THE TENTH PARTY CONGRESS**

The following is a summary of Lenin's remarks on 13 March 1921 to a conference of the delegates to the Tenth Congress of the RKP(b) – Supporters of the Platform of Ten.

Is the majority entitled to be a majority[?]. If it wants to be, then how should it be done[?]. For example, [of] three hundred, two hundred are the majority, and one hundred the minority. There arises the question of a split. A union is possible.

If the majority does not come to an arrangement, then the minority can win. This does happen. We are not a faction. We came as a faction, but we do not constitute a faction here. We should use our right in elections. In elections of delegates we have fought to win at the congress. And this we should do.

When the discussion got under way, then all saw the political mistake, and rightly so. It was a most dangerous discussion. The masses have taken it up, so they, too, have disagreements.

We must be firm, hard. Those who hesitate will join us.

Now as to Kronstadt. The danger there lies in the fact that their slogans are not Socialist-Revolutionary, but anarchistic.

An All-Russian Congress of Producers – this is not a Marxist but a petty bourgeois idea.

If you wish to introduce the opposition into the Central Committee to further its disintegration, then permit us not to permit it.

The 'Workers' Opposition' expresses the vacillations of the nonparty masses.

The 'Democratic Center' exists only in Moscow and unites only the intelligentsia. But it hinders work.

Moscow is the best city in the sense that it has a mass of intelligentsia, creators of theses, ex-officials, etc.

I have been accused: [']You are a son of a bitch for letting the discussion get out of hand.['] Well, try to stop Trotsky. How many divisions does one have to send against him?

The organization [apparat] is bad. Everyone hates the glavki. But no one agrees to disperse them. It is politics for the organization, not the organization ...

Our policy. From the point of view of the interests of the vanguard to the rear guard, of the whole class toward the peasantry [*sic*].

Yesterday about trade unions, and today to revamp the whole [military] command staff. Where are we to get the commissars[?].

We will come to terms with Trotsky.

The apparatus is for politics, not politics for the apparatus.

Trotsky wants to resign. Over the past three years I have had lots of resignations in my pockets. And I have let some of them just lie there in store. But Trotsky is a temperamental man with military experience. He is in love with the organization, but as for politics, he hasn't got a clue.

Richard Pipes, ed., with David Brandenberger,*The Unknown Lenin*, trans. Catherine A. Fitzpatrick, New Haven: Yale University Press, 1996, pp. 123–4.

CHRONOLOGY

1898	Formation of the Russian Social Democratic Workers' Party (RSDWP)
1902	Lenin publishes *What Is To Be Done?*, his blueprint for a revolutionary uprising
1903	Second Congress of RSDWP results in split between Bolsheviks and Mensheviks
1905	Revolution breaks out in Petrograd
1906	First Duma is convoked
1906–11	Premiership of Stolypin
1914–17	Russia in the First World War

1917

8–12 March	Revolution in Petrograd results in the collapse of the monarchy
12 March	Formation of a Provisional Government (Premier G. Lvov) and Petrograd Soviet of Workers' and Soldiers' Deputies
14 March	Order No. 1 leads to breakdown in army discipline
16 April	V.I. Lenin arrives in Petrograd (from Zurich)
17 April	Lenin delivers 'April Theses' denouncing Provisional Government
1 May	Foreign Minister P. Milyukov's support for continuation of Russian participation in the war sparks mass protests in Petrograd
4 May	New Cabinet formed; A. Kerensky becomes Minister of War
16 June	First All-Russian Congress of Soviets meets in Petrograd
16–17 July	Failed July Days uprising in Petrograd
19 July	Martial law declared; Trotsky arrested, Lenin goes into hiding
21 July	Kerensky becomes Prime Minister
25 August	Moscow State Conference
3 September	Riga falls to German army. General L. Kornilov commences revolt against Kerensky government; Kerensky releases Bolsheviks and allows Red Guards to gather arms
13 September	Bolshevik delegates comprise a majority in the Petrograd Soviet for the first time (L.D. Trotsky, Chairman)
18 September	Bolshevik delegates comprise a majority in the Moscow Soviet

8 October	Kerensky forms Third Coalition government (includes Kadets)
23 October	Central Committee of Bolsheviks approves uprising by 10 votes to 2
28 October	Petrograd Soviet forms a Military Revolutionary Committee
6–8 November	Armed uprising of Bolsheviks in Petrograd
7 November	Second Congress of Soviets begins in Petrograd
8 November	Lenin appears at the Congress and announces the formation of a new government, the Council of People's Commissars; Mensheviks and SRs leave assembly in protest
25 November	Elections held to the Constituent Assembly; the SRs achieve a majority
20 December	Lenin establishes the Commission to Combat Counter-Revolution and Sabotage (Cheka)

1918

18–20 January	Constituent Assembly meets in Petrograd and is dissolved by the Bolshevik government
21 January	Third All-Russian Congress of Soviets of Workers' and Soldiers' Deputies is convoked, merges with Congress of Peasants' Deputies
23 February	Decision made to form a Red Army
3 March	Treaty of Brest-Litovsk; Russia gives up most of European territory and withdraws from the First World War
March	Seat of government is moved from Petrograd to Moscow
13 May	Lenin breaks with western allies; civil war begins (lasts until early 1921)
May	Mensheviks and SRs banned from the Soviet Executive Committee; only the Left SRs remain in power with the Bolsheviks
6 July	Abortive uprising of Left SRs
16–17 July	Royal family murdered on the orders of Lenin, Ekaterinburg Oblast
30 August	Assassination of M.S. Uritsky, head of the Cheka in Petrograd; attempted assassination of Lenin in Moscow
5 September	Bolshevik government proclaims Red Terror

1921

1918–21	War Communism imposed
15 March	Tenth Party Congress introduces New Economic Policy
March	Kronstadt Revolt

1922

December	Formation of the Union of Soviet Socialist Republics

GLOSSARY

April Theses   A plan of action published by Lenin shortly after his return to Russia from Zurich in 1917. Advocated a takeover of power by the soviets. Initially the speech alienated leading Bolsheviks, but Lenin was able to persuade party members to support the plan.

Bolshevik Party   A faction of the Russian Social Democratic Party formed in 1903 under V.I. Lenin, who advanced the idea that a small conspiratorial group of committed revolutionaries was necessary to attain power in Russia. Though the name of the party means 'majority', the party was slightly smaller in size than the opposing Menshevik (or minority) faction. By 1917, the divisions had become solidified, and the Bolsheviks were in general more willing to circumvent Marxist doctrine and carry out an uprising when the moment seemed expedient.

Brest-Litovsk Treaty   A harsh peace treaty imposed on the Russians by the Central Powers in March 1918. It led to the temporary loss of much of the heartland of the European part of the former Russian Empire, including Poland, Finland and Ukraine.

Cheka   Extraordinary Commission to Combat Counter-Revolution and Sabotage, founded in December 1917 as a secret police organization under Feliks Dzerzhinsky. The forerunner of the latterday KGB and a key instrument during the Red Terror when it was given unlimited powers to detain and execute real and alleged opponents of the Bolshevik regime.

Duma   Russian parliament, first granted by Tsar Nikolay II in 1905 and convoked the following year. Four Dumas were elected between 1906 and 1917, with the franchise being progressively restricted. In March 1917 the Duma was dissolved, but its leaders met in an unofficial capacity to form the Provisional Government under Prince G.E. Lvov and, subsequently, A.F. Kerensky.

Kadets (Constitutional Democrats)   A Russian liberal party that was formed in 1905, made up for the most part of prominent Zemstvo members who wished to play a role in government policy-making. Its main goal (under its leader P. Milyukov) was for the convocation of a Constituent Assembly. In the First Duma, the Kadets were the largest political party, and although their numbers later dwindled, it was Milyukov and the Kadets who initially played the dominant role in the Provisional Government formed after the revolution of March 1917. With the polarization of Russian political life in this period, the 'liberal' Kadets found themselves on the Far Right of the political spectrum and became associated with reactionary views and ideas.

Kronstadt Revolt   An uprising by the sailors of the naval base just off Petrograd in March 1921. Hitherto the sailors had been the most militant and fanatical supporters of the Bolshevik regime, but believed that it had betrayed its promises. In particular the sailors demanded that political prisoners be released and that the government adhere to its platform.

Kulaks   Rich peasants. The term designated the class enemy, as opposed to the middle peasants (*serednyaks*) and poor peasants (*bednyaks*). Kulaks could also be farmers who hired labour, or who owned or leased machinery, or possessed land over norms established by the Bolsheviks.

Menshevik Party   In 1903 a group led by Y. Martov broke with a group led by Lenin at the Second Congress of the RSDWP in London. Several years later, the rift became permanent. The Mensheviks were orthodox Marxists who supported and ultimately participated in the Provisional Government in the belief that Russia must experience the full development of capitalism before a socialist revolution could take place.

New Economic Policy (NEP)   A policy introduced by Lenin at the Tenth Party Congress of March 1921 to replace War Communism. It replaced grain requisitions with a 'tax in kind', which allowed the peasants to dispense with surplus grain as they wished. As a result of the NEP, Russian agriculture recovered from the long years of warfare. Many Bolshevik leaders opposed the NEP as a retreat back to capitalism in the countryside. In 1928–29 Stalin abandoned the NEP and embarked on a policy of mass collectivization of the peasantry.

Octobrist Party   Formed in November 1905 in support of the Manifesto of 30 October 1905, granting Russia a Constitution. Comprised mainly of landowners and businessmen, their numbers rose in the Dumas, from 13 deputies in the First Duma to 154 in the Third (35 per cent of all deputies), falling to 97 in the Fourth Duma. The party played a pivotal role as 'centrists' on the political spectrum, particularly in the period 1912–17. The party was led by Aleksandr Guchkov.

Okhrana   The intelligence service (secret police) of Tsarist Russia.

Petrograd Soviet (Council)   A loose body representing workers, soldiers and subsequently peasants. First formed in 1905, it resurrected itself after the March 1917 revolution. Under SR and Menshevik control until September 1917, it was then taken over by a Bolshevik majority and played a pivotal role in the November Revolution. After the revolution, however, the soviets lost their authority to the party.

Provisional Government   The government formed from the Fourth Russian Duma in March 1917. The term 'provisional' was used because its leaders intended to form a permanent government following elections to the Constituent Assembly. In practice the government ruled under the close surveillance of the Petrograd Soviet, which had more support from the populace.

Russian Social Democratic Workers' Party (RSDWP, or Social Democrats)   Russian Marxist party, founded in 1898 at a congress in Minsk. Split in 1903 between Bolsheviks (led by V.I. Lenin) and Mensheviks (led by Y. Martov).

Social Revolutionary Party (SRs)   A peasant socialist party that was heir to the Populist movements of the nineteenth century and formed in 1900. Though it was the largest of the Russian socialist parties, it lacked organization and leadership. In 1917, a breakaway Left faction (Left SRs) formed an alliance with the Bolsheviks and ruled jointly with them for several months. In the short-lived Constituent Assembly (January 1918), the SRs won a majority of seats. An SR government was formed briefly during the civil war at Samara, comprised mainly of members of the dissolved Assembly.

Trudoviki   A peasant-based party formed in April 1906 from deputies of the First Duma. Advocated the transferral of landowners' estates to the peasants and an agrarian reform that would see the nationalization of all remaining land. They had over 90 deputies in the First Duma, but by the period of the Fourth Duma (1912–17), they had declined to ten, led by Aleksandr Kerensky (who subsequently defected to the SRs.

War Communism   An economic system introduced by Lenin's government in mid-1918 which combined the nationalization and centralized control of industry with a harsh policy of grain requisitions in the countryside and the division of the peasantry according to an artificially created class structure. Under War Communism the Bolshevik regime suffered from acute shortages of food and supplies, and a famine broke out in many areas of Russia in 1921. The system was abandoned in March 1921.

Zemstvo   A village assembly founded in 1864 by Tsar Aleksandr II to introduce some self-government in the regions of Russia. They were divided into district zemstva, which in turn elected the provincial zemstva. The nobility had disproportionate influence and control over the zemstva, but the institution proved durable, especially in areas such as education, health and welfare in the localities. In 1870, city zemstva were also established and were responsible for the maintenance of roads and water supply. Though the zemstva did not acquire the political authority that might have solidified their power, they proved a breeding ground for liberal ideas.

WHO'S WHO

Aleksandra Feodorovna (1872–1918)   The last empress of Russia, German by extraction, she was a grand-daughter of Queen Victoria of England, and was English by upbringing. Became a devout follower of the Orthodox faith, but was unpopular among the public, especially after the outbreak of war in 1914 and when she and Rasputin assumed control of affairs of state in the absence of Tsar Nikolay. Executed on Lenin's orders in July 1918.

Antonov-Ovseenko, Vladimir A. (1884–1939)   A native of Chernihiv, Ukraine, who joined the Russian Social Democratic Party in 1903. After a short sojourn in France where he associated with the Mensheviks, he joined the Bolshevik Party in May 1917 upon his return to Russia and was secretary of the Military Revolutionary Committee in the November uprising. Commanded the Ukrainian Front during the civil war. His later career was as Russian ambassador to Czechoslovakia (1925), Lithuania (1928) and Poland (1930 onward).

Bubnov, Andrey S. (1883–1940)   A Russian Social Democrat from Ivanovo-Voznesensk. Worked for the Bolshevik leadership in Moscow after the March 1917 Revolution. Became a leader of the Bolshevik government in Ukraine in March 1918, and also played a prominent role in the repression of the Kronstadt uprising of March 1921.

Budenny, Semen M. (1883–1973)   A civil war hero who joined the Communist Party in 1919. A veteran of the Russo-Japanese War of 1904–5 and the First World War. Commanded a cavalry division at Tsaritsyn (later Stalingrad, and currently Volgograd). From November 1919 commanded the First Cavalry Army, which recaptured the Donbass region from Denikin's White army. Also played a prominent role in the defeat of Wrangel. Became a Marshal of the Soviet Union in 1935 and a Hero of the Soviet Union in 1958.

Denikin, Anton I. (1872–1947)   A lieutenant-general in the tsarist army who became Chief Commander of the White army during the civil war. Participated in the failed Kornilov Revolt of 1917 and at the end of the year was one of the founders of the Volunteer Army, which he led after Kornilov's death in April 1918. In the summer of 1919 his army threatened Moscow but he was defeated in the North Caucasus in March 1920 and fled to the Crimea, subsequently relinquishing command to Wrangel. Emigrated abroad in this same year.

Dybenko, Pavel E. (1889–1938)   Born into a peasant family from the Chernihiv region, he joined the Russian Social Democratic Party in 1912. Arrested as an anti-war activist and freed during the March 1917 Revolution. After the Bolshevik uprising he became People's Commissar for the Navy, then worked in the Bolshevik underground in Crimea and Ukraine in the summer of 1918. Played a prominent role in the civil war in Tsaritsyn and Crimea. A victim of Stalin's purges.

Dzerzhinsky, Feliks E. (1877–1926)   Born in the Vilna gubernia of Poland and a fanatical activist in the Polish, Lithuanian and Russian revolutionary movements. Frequently arrested, he took part in the Fourth Congress of the RSDWP in Stockholm in 1906 where he first met Lenin. One of the founders of the Red Guards. Became the Chairman of the Cheka upon its founding on 20 December 1917 and remains best known as the creator of the Soviet secret police (the modern-day KGB).

Guchkov, Aleksandr I.(1862–1936)   Founder and leader of the Octobrist Party. Became the Chairman of the Duma in March 1910, but resigned a year later in protest against Stolypin's land reform. Became Minister of War and Naval Affairs in the Provisional Government of 1917 but resigned two months later. Emigrated to Berlin in 1918.

Kerensky, Aleksandr F. (1881–1970)   Leader of the Trudoviki party between 1912 and 1917. In March 1917 he was the only leader to play a role in both the Petrograd Soviet and the Provisional Government. He held the posts of Minister of Justice (March), Minister of War (May) and Prime Minister (July to early November). Fled from Petrograd at the time of the Bolshevik uprising and eventually emigrated to the United States where he embarked on an academic career.

Kolchak, Aleksandr V. (1873–1920)   Admiral. Born in St Petersburg into a family of naval officers, he became the commander of the Black Sea Fleet in July 1916. Went to the USA after the February Revolution, but returned to the Russian Far East in late 1917. On 4 November 1918 became the war and naval minister of the Siberian government in opposition to the Bolsheviks. On 18 November he was appointed the 'Supreme Ruler of Russia' (dictatorship) with the support of the western allies. Detained by the Czechs in December 1919, he was handed over to to the Red leaders in Irkutsk and executed.

Kollontay, Aleksandra M. (1872–1952)   Petersburg-born professional revolutionary and feminist who was also a general's daughter. Between 1908 and 1917 she took part in socialist movements in various countries of Europe and the USA. She returned to Petrograd in March 1917 and earned a reputation as a talented orator. A member of the first Bolshevik government, she became associated with the Left Communists in 1918 and spent her later years as an ambassador to Norway (1923–26 and 1927–30), Mexico (1926–27) and Sweden (1930–45).

Kornilov, Lavr G. (1870–1918)   Noted Russian general who spent much of his early career in the Far East. Appointed Commander-in-Chief by Kerensky in August 1917, he at once tried to establish a military dictatorship (whether with or without Kerensky's consent has been much debated). His rebellion was defeated, but he was subsequently one of the founders of the Volunteer Army against the new Bolshevik regime and its first leader.

Krupskaya, Nadezhda K. (1869–1939)   Born in St Petersburg and joined Marxist circles in that city from 1890 onward. Met Lenin in 1894. In 1898 both she and Lenin were exiled to Ufa for three years and married there. In 1901 she emigrated to Munich and became an editorial secretary on the newspaper *Iskra* and subsequently had the same position on the newspaper *Vpered* (from 1904). Remained a devout partner and follower of Lenin throughout his life.

Krylenko, Nikolay V. (1885–1938)   A native of Smolensk region who was one of the leaders of the revolutionary movement of 1904–5. In 1913 worked in St Petersburg as a Bolshevik deputy of the Duma and on the newspaper *Pravda*. Played an active role in the November 1917 uprising as a member of the Military Revolutionary Committee. A member of the first Bolshevik government as the Commander-in-Chief and Commissar of Military Affairs. Later became an organizer of the Soviet lawcourts, Chief Prosecutor of the Russian Federation (1922–31), Minister of Justice of the RSFSR (1931–36) and USSR (1936–38).

Lenin, V.I. (1870–1924)   Born Vladimir Ilich Ulyanov into a petty noble family in Simbirsk. Bolshevik leader, who organized the November 1917 uprising and became the head of the first Soviet government (Council of People's Commissars). After his death in January 1924, he was transformed by Stalin and others into a virtual deity, and his embalmed corpse remains in a mausoleum in Moscow's Red Square.

Lunacharsky, Anatoly V. (1875–1933)   Born in Poltava into the family of a local official, he was involved in Marxist work from 1895 onward. Had close links with the early Liberation of Labour group and with Grigorii Plekhanov personally. After a period of exile he emigrated to Geneva (1904) and worked on the Bolshevik newspapers *Vpered* and *Proletariy*. A writer and publicist, he returned to Russia in May 1917, and after the November uprising he held the position of People's Commissar of Education from 1917 to 1929.

Lvov, Prince G.E. (1861–1925)   A nobleman and great landowner, and chairman of the Zemstvo Union during the First World War, he became the first Prime Minister of the Provisional Government formed in March 1917; resigned in July 1917.

Martov, I. (1873–1923)   Born Yuly Osipovich Tsederbaum. Originally a member of the Jewish Bund, he became a close colleague of Lenin as an editor of *Iskra* in 1899. In 1903 at the Second Congress of the Russian Social Democrats he opposed Lenin's motion to form a small and tightly disciplined party and subsequently became the leader of the opposing faction, the Mensheviks (Minority). He supported the policy of peace without victory during the First World War and was loyal to the Bolsheviks during the civil war. The latter part of his life was spent in Germany (1920–23).

Milyukov, Pavel N. (1859–1943)   Historian and leader of the Kadet Party. Supporting liberal causes, he returned to Russia in 1905 after a period of European exile and was one of the main organizers of the Kadet Party, becoming chairman of its Central Committee in 1907. Became a deputy in the Third and Fourth Dumas. Though he tried unsuccessfully to preserve the monarchy, he was appointed Minister of Foreign Affairs in the first Cabinet of the Provisional Government in 1917, but was forced to resign after sending a secret note to the allies on 14 May outlining Russia's continuing support for a war until final victory. Emigrated to London in 1921 and moved to Paris a year later.

Nikolay (Nicholas II) (1868–1918)   A Romanov and the last tsar of Russia. Executed on Lenin's orders on 16–17 July 1918.

Rasputin, Grigory Yefimovich (1872–1916)   A half-literate wanderer who preached a form of religion that combined fervour with deviation and wielded an inordinate influence over the Russian royal family between 1911 and 1916.

Rodzianko, Mikhail (1859–1924)   One of the leaders of the Octobrist Party (see above), a prominent politician of 1917, and a noted monarchist. A landowner from Ekaterinoslav district, he became a deputy of the Third and Fourth Dumas, and Chairman of the Duma after 1911. After the October Revolution, he ultimately joined the White forces and emigrated to Yugoslavia in 1920.

Skoropadsky, Pavlo P. (1873–1945)   Ukrainian landowner and commander of a cavalry division during the First World War. Elected Hetman of Ukraine at a Congress in Kyiv when Ukraine was under German-Austrian occupation. After the defeat of Germany in the First World War he fled to that country in December 1918.

Stalin, Iosif V. (1878–1953)   Georgian Bolshevik who played a significant role in the November uprising and became the Commissar for Nationalities in the first Bolshevik government. Subsequently played a prominent role in the Tsaritsyn region during the civil war and came into frequent conflict with his Commander-in-Chief, Trotsky. After Lenin's death in January 1924, Stalin created a strong power base using the party bureaucracy and using Lenin's legacy to establish a creed of party infallibility and remove his rivals. Through his position as General Secretary, Stalin was dictator of the Soviet Union from 1928 to 1953 and responsible for massive purges of the population, industrialization and the collectivization of peasant agriculture.

Sverdlov, Yakob M. (1885–1919)   A native of Nizhny Novgorod, he joined the Russian Social Democrats in 1901. In 1905 led the Ekaterinburg committee of the party. A close and loyal follower of Lenin and a gifted administrator, he spent the spring and summer of 1917 in Ekaterinburg, but was one of the organizers of the November 1917 uprising and long-time secretary of the Bolshevik Party until his premature death in 1919.

Tereshchenko, Mikhail I. (1886–??)   A millionaire sugar manufacturer based in Ukraine, who has remained an obscure figure. Became the Minister of Finance of the Provisional Government in March 1917, and subsequently Minister of Foreign Affairs from May until October. Supported the Whites and foreign intervention during the civil war.

Trotsky, L.D. (1879–1940)   Born Lev Davidovich Bronstein and raised in southern Ukraine. A harsh critic of Lenin and the Bolsheviks in 1903. Chairman of the Petrograd Soviet in late 1905 and again in September 1917. Close associate of Lenin from May 1917 onward when he returned to Russia from New York. The main organizer of the November 1917 uprising and founder of the Red Army. A brilliant orator and writer, he was to prove inept at political intrigue and was outmanoeuvred by Stalin after Lenin's death. Ultimately exiled from the Soviet Union, and was assassinated by a Stalinist agent in Mexico in 1940.

Uritsky, Moisey S. (1873–1918)   A native of Cherkasy, Ukraine, and a member of the Bolshevik Party from 1917. Gravitated to the Menshevik Party after the 1903 split in the Russian Social Democrats. After three years abroad he returned to Russia after the March Revolution and was a member of the Interdistrict Group that was incorporated into the Bolshevik Party. In 1918 he became the leader of the Petrograd Cheka and was assassinated by an SR terrorist on 30 August 1918.

Wrangel, Petr N. (1878–1928)   A baron from the Baltic region who led the Volunteer (White) Army in the Caucasus (Spring 1919) and the Kharkiv area (December 1919). After being involved in intrigues against Denikin, he was dismissed from his command and went abroad. After the collapse of Denikin's armies, Wrangel replaced him as Commander-in-Chief of all the White armies in April 1920 and proved a capable leader, although the military situation was now irretrievable. Like other White leaders, he favoured a military dictatorship and the restoration of estates to the great landowners.

Yudenich, Nikolay N. (1862–1933)   An infantry general in the First World War, he became the White commander in the north-west during the civil war, having earlier (autumn 1918) emigrated from Russia to Finland, and then Estonia. After the defeat of part of his army not far from Petrograd (October–November 1919), he returned to Estonia and eventually to Britain.

Zinoviev, Grigory Yevseevich (1883–1936)   Born Gershon Radomylsky. A close colleague of Lenin, who heralded from a poor Jewish family and lacked a formal education. He joined the Bolshevik faction after 1903 and was a close associate of Lenin in the period 1906–17. However, in the period prior to the November Revolution, he and his colleague Lev Kamenev opposed a Bolshevik uprising and resigned for a short time from the Central Committee of the party. However, he later became the chairman of the executive committee of the Communist International (Comintern), partly as a result of his oratorical skills After Lenin's death, he and Kamenev formed a 'troika' with Stalin to ensure the defeat of Trotsky, but by the end of 1926 he had been himself removed from both the politburo and the Comintern, and in 1927 he lost his party membership. He fell victim to the Stalin Purges in 1936, allegedly for his role in the assassination of the Leningrad party chief, Sergei Kirov.

BIBLIOGRAPHY

DOCUMENTS AND EYEWITNESS ACCOUNTS

1   Bing, Edward J., ed. *The Secret Letters of the Last Tsar*. New York: Longmans, Green and Co., 1938.

2   Brovkin, Vladimir, ed. and trans. *Dear Comrades: Menshevik Reports on the Bolshevik Revolution and Civil War*. Stanford, CA: Hoover Institution Press, 1991.

3   Bunyan, James, ed. *Intervention, Civil War and Communism in Russia, April–December 1918: Documents and Materials*. Baltimore, MD: Johns Hopkins University Press, 1936.

4   Bunyan, James and H.H. Fisher, eds. *The Bolshevik Revolution of 1917–1918: Documents and Materials*. Stanford, CA: Stanford University Press, 1934.

5   Chamberlin, William Henry. *The Russian Revolution, 1817–1921*, 2 vols. New York: Macmillan, 1957.

6   Cracraft, James, ed. *Major Problems in the History of Imperial Russia*. Lexington, MA: D.C. Heath and Company, 1994.

7   Dune, Edward M. *Notes of a Red Guard*, ed. and trans. Diane P. Koenker and S.A. Smith. Urbana, IL: University of Illinois Press, 1993.

8   Frank, Pierre, ed. *Kronstadt: By V.I. Lenin and Leon Trotsky*. New York: Monad Press, 1979.

9   Homberger, Eric and John Biggart, eds. *John Reed and the Russian Revolution: Uncollected Articles, Letters and Speeches on Russia, 1917–1920*. New York: St Martin's Press, 1992.

10 Horsburgh Power, Anna, ed. *Memories of the Revolution: Russian Women Remember*. New York: Routledge, 1993.

11 Kerensky, Aleksandr. *The Crucifixion of Liberty*, trans. G. Kerensky from the unpublished Russian manuscript. New York: John Day, 1934.

12 Lenin, V.I. *Selected Works in Three Volumes*. Moscow: Progress Publishers, 1973.

13 Milyukov, Paul. *Political Memoirs 1905–1917*. Ann Arbor, MI: University of Michigan Press, 1967.

14 Pipes, Richard, ed. *The Unknown Lenin: From the Secret Archive*, with the assistance of David Brandenberger, trans. Catherine A. Fitzpatrick. Annals of Communism. New Haven, CT: Yale University Press, 1996.

15 Reed, John. *Ten Days that Shook the World*. New York: Boni and Liveright, 1919.

16 Riddell, John, ed. *Founding the Communist International. Proceedings and Documents of the First Congress, March 1919*. London: Pathfinder Press, 1987.

17 Sukhanov, N.N. *The Russian Revolution, 1917: Eyewitness Account*, 2 vols. London: Oxford University Press, 1955.

18 Trotsky, Leon. *The History of the Russian Revolution*, 3 vols. New York: Simon and Schuster, 1932.

GENERAL HISTORIES

19 Mackenzie, David and Michael W. Curran. *A History of Russia, the Soviet Union, and Beyond*, 4th edn. Belmont, CA: Wadsworth Publishing Company, 1993.

20 Service, Robert. *A History of Twentieth-Century Russia*. Cambridge, MA: Harvard University Press, 1998.

21 Seton-Watson, Hugh. *The Russian Empire 1801–1917*. Oxford: Clarendon Press, 1967.

PRE-REVOLUTION

22 Geifman, Anna. *Thou Shalt Kill: Revolutionary Terrorism in Russia, 1894– 1917*. Princeton, NJ: Princeton University Press, 1993.

23 Rogger, Hans. *Russia in the Age of Modernisation and Revolution, 1881– 1917*. New York: Longman, 1983.

24 Saunders, David. *Russia in the Age of Reaction and Reform 1801–1881*. London: Longman, 1992.

25 Wildman, Allan K. *The End of the Russian Imperial Army*. Volume 1: *The Old Army and the Soldiers' Revolt, March–April 1917*. Princeton, NJ: Princeton University Press, 1980. Volume 2: *The Road to Soviet Power and Peace*. Princeton, NJ: Princeton University Press, 1987.

26 Zimmerman, Judith E. *Mid-Passage: Aleksandr Herzen and European Revolution, 1847–1852*. Pitt Series in Russian and East European Studies, No. 10, Pittsburgh, PA: University of Pittsburgh Press.

THE ROYAL FAMILY

27 Crawford, Donald and Rosemary Crawford. *Michael and Natasha: The Life and Love of the Last Tsar of Russia*. London: Weidenfeld and Nicolson, 1997.

28 Lieven, Dominic. *Nicholas II: Tsar of all the Russias*. London: Pimlico, 1993.

29 Steinberg, Mark D. and Vladimir Khrustalev. *The Fall of the Romanovs: Political Dreams and Personal Struggles in a Time of Revolution*. New Haven, CT: Yale University Press, 1995.

30 Verner, Andrew N. *The Crisis of Russian Autocracy: Nikolay II and the 1905 Revolution*. Princeton, NJ: Princeton University Press, 1990.

BIOGRAPHIES

31 Daniels, Robert V. *Trotsky, Stalin, and Socialism*. Boulder, CO: Westview Press, 1991.

32 Fuhrmann, Joseph T. *Rasputin: A Life*. New York: Praeger, 1990.

33   Kingston-Mann, Esther. *Lenin and the Problem of Marxist Peasant Revolution*. New York: Oxford University Press, 1983.
34   Kirschke, Melissa. *Paul Miliukov and the Quest for a Liberal Russia, 1880–1918*. Ithaca, NY: Cornell University Press, 1996.
35   Pomper, Phillip. *Lenin, Trotsky, and Stalin: The Intelligentsia and Power*. New York: Columbia University Press, 1990.
36   Service, Robert. *Lenin: A Political Life,* 3 vols. Bloomington, IN: Indiana University Press, 1985, 1991 and 1995.
37   Slusser, Robert M. *Stalin in October: The Man Who Missed the Revolution*. Baltimore, MD: Johns Hopkins University Press, 1987.
38   Tumarkin, Nina. *Lenin Lives! The Lenin Cult in Soviet Russia*. Cambridge, MA: Harvard University Press, 1983.
39   Volkogonov, Dmitri. *Lenin: Life and Legacy*, ed. and trans Harold Skulman. New York: Free Press, 1994.
40   Williams, Robert C. *The Other Bolsheviks: Lenin and his Critics, 1904–1914*. Bloomington, IN: Indiana University Press, 1986.

THE 1905 REVOLUTION

41   Ascher, Abraham. *The Revolution of 1905: Russia in Disarray*. Stanford, CA: Stanford University Press, 1988.
42   Ascher, Abraham. *The Revolution of 1905: Authority Restored*. Stanford, CA: Stanford University Press, 1992.
43   Bushnell, John. *Mutiny Amid Repression: Russian Soldiers in the Revolution of 1905–06*. Indiana–Michigan Series in Russian and East-European Studies. Bloomington, IN: Indiana University Press, 1985.
44   Edelman, Robert. *Proletarian Peasants: The Revolution of 1905 in Russia's Southwest*. Ithaca, NY: Cornell University Press, 1987.
45   Rawson, Don C. *Russian Rightists and the Revolution of 1905*. Cambridge Russian, Soviet and Post-Soviet Studies, No. 95. New York: Cambridge University Press, 1995.
46   Rice, Christopher. *Russian Workers and the Socialist-Revolutionary Party through the Revolution of 1905–07*. New York: St Martin's Press, 1988.
47   Shanin, Teodor. *The Roots of Otherness: Russia's Turn of the Century*. Volume 1: *Russia as a 'Developing Society'*. Volume 2: *Russia, 1905–07: Revolution as a Moment of Truth*. New Haven, CT: Yale University Press, 1986.
48   Surh, Gerald D. *1905 in St Petersburg: Labor, Society, and Revolution*. Stanford, CA: Stanford University Press, 1989.

THE REVOLUTIONS OF 1917

49   Basil, John D. *The Mensheviks in the Revolution of 1917*. Columbus, OH: Slavica Publishers, 1983.
50   Brovkin, Vladimir N. *The Mensheviks After October: Socialist Opposition and the Rise of the Bolshevik Dictatorship*. Ithaca, NY: Cornell University Press, 1987.

51   Carr, E.H. *The Bolshevik Revolution 1917–1923 (Part 1): A History of Soviet Russia*, Volume 1. London: Macmillan, 1960.
52   Daniels, Robert V. *Red October: The Bolshevik Revolution of 1917*. New York: Secker & Warburg, 1967.
53   Figes, Orlando. *A People's Tragedy: The Russian Revolution 1891–1924*. London: Jonathan Cape, 1996.
54   Fitzpatrick, Sheila. *The Russian Revolution 1917–1932*. New York: Oxford University Press, 1984.
55   Galili, Ziva. *The Menshevik Leaders in the Russian Revolution: Social Realities and Political Strategies*. Studies of the Harriman Institute. Princeton, NJ: Princeton University Press, 1989.
56   Gleason, Abbott, *et al.*, eds. *Bolshevik Culture: Experiment and Order in the Russian Revolution*. Studies of the Kennan Institute for Advanced Russian Studies, the Wilson Center, No. 5. Bloomington, IN: Indiana University Press, 1985.
57   *The Great October Socialist Revolution*. Moscow: Progress Publishers, 1977.
58   Harding, Neil. *Leninism*. Durham, TX: Duke University Press, 1996.
59   Hasegawa, Tsuyoshu. *The February Revolution: Petrograd 1917*. Seattle, WA: University of Washington Press, 1981.
60   Heenan, Louise Erwin. *Russian Democracy's Fatal Blunder: The Summer Offensive of 1917*. New York: Praeger of Greenwood Press, 1987.
61   Katkov, George. *Russia 1917: The Kornilov Affair: Kerensky and the Breakup of the Russian Army*. London: Longman, 1980.
62   Koenker, Diane and William G. Rosenberg. *Strikes and Revolution in Russia, 1917*. Princeton, NJ: Princeton University Press, 1989.
63   Kowalski, Ronald I. *The Bolshevik Party in Conflict: The Left Communist Opposition of 1918*. Pittsburgh, PA: Pittsburgh University Press, 1991.
64   Liebman, Marcel. *The Russian Revolution*. New York: Vintage Books, 1970.
65   Lyandres, Semion. *The Bolsheviks' 'German Gold' Revisited: An Inquiry into the 1917 Accusations*. Carl Beck Papers in Russian and East European Studies, No. 1106. Pittsburgh, PA: Center for Russian and East European Studies, 1995.
66   McDaniel, Tim. *Autocracy, Capitalism, and Revolution in Russia*. Berkeley, CA: University of California Press, 1988.
67   Moynahan, Brian. *Comrades: 1917 – Russia in Revolution*. Boston, MA: Little, Brown, 1992.
68   Pipes, Richard. *The Russian Revolution*. New York: Alfred A. Knopf, 1990.
69   Raleigh, Donald J. *Revolution on the Volga: 1917 in Saratov*. Ithaca, NY: Cornell University Press, 1986.
70   Schapiro, Leonard. *The Russian Revolutions of 1917: The Origins of Modern Communism*. New York: Basic Books, 1984.
71   Thompson, John M. *Revolutionary Russia, 1917*. New York: Scribners, 1981.
72   Ulam, Adam B. *The Bolsheviks: The Intellectual, Personal and Political History of the Triumph of Communism in Russia*. New York: Macmillan, 1965.
73   Weber, Max, *et al. The Russian Revolutions*. Ithaca, NY: Cornell University Press, 1995.

SOCIAL HISTORIES

74   Atkinson, Dorothy. *The End of the Russian Land Commune*. Stanford, CA: Stanford University Press, 1983.

75   Bonnell, Victoria E. *Roots of Rebellion: Workers' Politics and Organizations in St Petersburg and Moscow, 1900–1914*. Berkeley and Los Angeles, CA: University of California Press, 1983.

76   Ferro, Marc. *October 1917: A Social History of the Russian Revolution*. London: Routledge and Kegan Paul, 1980.

77   Glickman, Rose L. *Russian Factory Women: Workplace and Society, 1880–1914*. Berkeley and Los Angeles, CA: University of California Press, 1984.

78   Hutchison, John F. *Politics and Public Health in Revolutionary Russia, 1890–1918*. Henry E. Sigerist Series in the History of Medicine. Baltimore, MD: Johns Hopkins University Press, 1990.

79   Kaiser, Daniel H. *The Workers' Revolution in Russia, 1917: The View from Below*. New York: Cambridge University Press, 1987.

80   Lih, Lars T. *Bread and Authority in Russia, 1914–1921*. Berkeley and Los Angeles, CA: University of California Press, 1990.

81   Mally, Lynn. *Culture of the Future: The Proletkult Movement in Revolutionary Russia*. Berkeley and Los Angeles, CA: University of California Press, 1990.

82   McKean, Robert B. *St Petersburg between the Revolutions: Workers and Revolutionaries, June 1907–February 1917*. New Haven, CT: Yale University Press, 1990.

83   Porter, Cathy. *Women in Revolutionary Russia*. New York: Cambridge University Press, 1987.

84   Read, Christopher. *From Tsar to Soviets: The Russian People and Their Revolution, 1917–1921*. New York: Oxford University Press, 1996.

85   Remington, Thomas F. *Building Socialism in Bolshevik Russia: Ideology and Industrial Organization, 1917–1921*. Pittsburgh, PA: University of Pittsburgh Press, 1984.

86   Siegelbaum, Lewis H. *The Politics of Industrial Mobilization in Russia, 1914–17: A Study of the War Industries Committees*. New York: St Martin's Press, 1983.

87   Smith, S.A. *Red Petrograd: Revolution in the Factories, 1917–1918*. New York: Cambridge University Press, 1983.

88   Stites, Richard. *Revolutionary Dreams: Utopian Vision and Experimental Life in the Russian Revolution*. New York: Oxford University Press, 1989.

89   Suny, Ronald Grigor. 'Toward a Social History of the October Revolution'. *American Historical Review*, Vol. 99, No. 1 (February 1983): 31–52.

90   Wade, Rex A. *Red Guards and Workers' Militias in the Russian Revolution*. Stanford, CA: Stanford University Press, 1984.

91   White, Stephen. *The Bolshevik Poster*. New Haven, CT: Yale University Press, 1989.

92   Yaney, George. *The Urge to Mobilize: Agrarian Reform in Russia, 1861–1930*. Urbana, IL: University of Illinois Press, 1982.

ASSESSMENTS AND DISCUSSIONS

93 Acton, Edward. *Rethinking the Russian Revolution*. New York: Edward Arnold, 1990.

94 Adams, Arthur E. *Imperial Russia After 1861: Peaceful Modernization or Revolution?* Problems in European Civilization. Boston, MA: D.C. Heath and Company, 1965.

95 Burbank, Jane. *Intelligentsia and Revolution: Russian Views of Bolshevism, 1917–1922*. New York: Oxford University Press, 1986.

96 Frankel, Edith R., Jonathan, Frankel, and Baruch Knei Paz. *Revolution in Russia: Reassessments of 1917*. New York: Cambridge University Press, 1992.

97 Geyer, Dietrich. *The Russian Revolution: Historical Problems and Perspectives*. New York: St Martin's Press, 1987.

98 Kolonitskii, Boris I. 'Antibourgeois Propaganda and Anti-"Burzhui" Consciousness in 1917'. *Russian Review*, Vol. 53, No. 2 (April 1994): 183–96.

99 Schapiro, Leonard. *Russian Studies*. London: Penguin Books, 1988.

100 Suny, Ronald and Arthur Adams, eds. *The Russian Revolution and Bolshevik Victory*, 3rd edn. Problems in European Civilization. Lexington, MA: DC Heath and Company, 1990.

NON-RUSSIANS

101 Hunczak, Taras, ed. *The Ukraine 1917–1921: A Study in Revolution*. Cambridge, MA: Harvard University Press, 1977.

102 Pinkus, Benjamin. *The Jews of the Soviet Union: The History of a National Minority*. Cambridge: Cambridge University Press, 1988.

103 Reshetar, John. *The Ukrainian Revolution 1917–1920*. Princeton, NJ: Princeton University Press, 1950.

104 Suny, Ronald G. *The Making of the Georgian Nation*. Bloomington, IN: University of Indiana Press, 1988.

105 Vakar, Nicholas P. *Belorussia: The Making of a Nation*. Cambridge, MA: Harvard University Press, 1954.

CIVIL WAR

106 Benvenuti, Francesco. *The Bolsheviks and the Red Army, 1918–1922*. New York: Cambridge University Press, 1988.

107 Debo, Richard K. *Revolution and Survival: The Foreign Policy of Soviet Russia, 1917–1918*. Buffalo, NY: University of Toronto Press, 1979.

108 Figes, Orlando. *Peasant Russia, Civil War: The Volga Countryside in Revolution, 1917–1921*. New York: Clarendon Press of Oxford University Press, 1989.

109 Getzler, Israel. *Kronstadt, 1917–1921: The Fate of a Soviet Democracy*. New York: Cambridge University Press, 1983.

110 Lincoln, W. Bruce. *Red Victory: A History of the Russian Civil War*. New York: Simon and Schuster, 1989.

111 Malle, Silvana. *The Economic Organization of War Communism, 1918–1921*. New York: Cambridge University Press, 1985.

112   Mawdsley, E. *The Russian Civil War.* London: Allen & Unwin, 1987.

113   Pereira, N.G.O. *White Siberia: The Politics of Civil War.* Montreal: McGill-Queen's University Press, 1996.

114   Sakwa, Richard. *Soviet Communism in Power: A Study of Moscow During the Civil War, 1918–1921.* New York: St Martin's Press, 1988.

115   Smele, Jonathan D. *Civil War in Siberia: The Anti-Bolshevik Government of Admiral Kolchak, 1918–1920.* Cambridge: Cambridge University Press, 1996.

116   Swain, Geoffrey. *The Origins of the Russian Civil War.* London: Longman, 1996.

REVIEWS AND REVIEW ARTICLES

117   Getzler, Israel. 'Richard Pipes's "Revisionist" History of the Russian Revolution'. *Slavonic and East European Review*, Vol. 70, No. 1 (January 1992): 111–26.

118   Kenez, Peter. 'The Prosecution of Soviet History: A Critique of Richard Pipes' *The Russian Revolution*'. *Russian Review*, Vol. 50, No. 3 (1991): 345–51.

119   Suny, Ronald Grigor. 'Revision and Retreat in the Historiography of 1917: Social History and Its Critics'. *Russian Review*, Vol. 53, No. 2 (April 1994): 165–82.

INDEX

SEMINAR STUDIES IN HISTORY

General Editors: Clive Emsley & Gordon Martel

The series was founded by Patrick Richardson in 1966. Between 1980 and 1996 Roger Lockyer edited the series before handing over to Clive Emsley (Professor of History at the Open University) and Gordon Martel (Professor of International History at the University of Northern British Columbia, Canada and Senior Research Fellow at De Montfort University).

MEDIEVAL ENGLAND

The Pre-Reformation Church in England 1400–1530 (Second edition)
Christopher Harper-Bill   0 582 28989 0

Lancastrians and Yorkists: The Wars of the Roses
David R Cook   0 582 35384 X

TUDOR ENGLAND

Henry VII (Third edition)
Roger Lockyer & Andrew Thrush   0 582 20912 9

Henry VIII (Second edition)
M D Palmer   0 582 35437 4

Tudor Rebellions (Fourth edition)
Anthony Fletcher & Diarmaid MacCulloch   0 582 28990 4

The Reign of Mary I (Second edition)
Robert Tittler   0 582 06107 5

Early Tudor Parliaments 1485–1558
Michael A R Graves   0 582 03497 3

The English Reformation 1530–1570
W J Sheils   0 582 35398 X

Elizabethan Parliaments 1559–1601 (Second edition)
Michael A R Graves   0 582 29196 8

England and Europe 1485–1603 (Second edition)
Susan Doran   0 582 28991 2

The Church of England 1570–1640
Andrew Foster   0 582 35574 5

STUART BRITAIN

Social Change and Continuity: England 1550–1750 (Second edition)
Barry Coward   0 582 29442 8

James I (Second edition)
S J Houston   0 582 20911 0

The English Civil War 1640–1649
Martyn Bennett   0 582 35392 0

Charles I, 1625–1640
Brian Quintrell   0 582 00354 7

The English Republic 1649–1660 (Second edition)
Toby Barnard   0 582 08003 7

Radical Puritans in England 1550–1660
R J Acheson   0 582 35515 X

The Restoration and the England of Charles II (Second edition)
John Miller   0 582 29223 9

The Glorious Revolution (Second edition)
John Miller   0 582 29222 0

EARLY MODERN EUROPE

The Renaissance (Second edition)
Alison Brown   0 582 30781 3

The Emperor Charles V
Martyn Rady   0 582 35475 7

French Renaissance Monarchy: Francis I and Henry II (Second edition)
Robert Knecht   0 582 28707 3

The Protestant Reformation in Europe
Andrew Johnston   0 582 07020 1

The French Wars of Religion 1559–1598 (Second edition)
Robert Knecht   0 582 28533 X

Phillip II
Geoffrey Woodward   0 582 07232 8

The Thirty Years' War
Peter Limm   0 582 35373 4

Louis XIV
Peter Campbell   0 582 01770 X

Spain in the Seventeenth Century
Graham Darby   0 582 07234 4

Peter the Great
William Marshall   0 582 00355 5

EUROPE 1789–1918

Britain and the French Revolution
Clive Emsley   0 582 36961 4

Revolution and Terror in France 1789–1795 (Second edition)
D G Wright   0 582 00379 2

Napoleon and Europe
D G Wright   0 582 35457 9

Nineteenth-Century Russia: Opposition to Autocracy
Derek Offord   0 582 35767 5

The Constitutional Monarchy in France 1814–48
Pamela Pilbeam   0 582 31210 8

The 1848 Revolutions (Second edition)
Peter Jones   0 582 06106 7

The Italian Risorgimento
M Clark   0 582 00353 9

Bismark & Germany 1862–1890 (Second edition)
D G Williamson   0 582 29321 9

Imperial Germany 1890–1918
Ian Porter, Ian Armour and Roger Lockyer   0 582 03496 5

The Dissolution of the Austro-Hungarian Empire 1867–1918 (Second edition)
John W Mason   0 582 29466 5

Second Empire and Commune: France 1848–1871 (Second edition)
William H C Smith   0 582 28705 7

France 1870–1914 (Second edition)
Robert Gildea   0 582 29221 2

The Scramble for Africa (Second edition)
M E Chamberlain   0 582 36881 2

Late Imperial Russia 1890–1917
John F Hutchinson   0 582 32721 0

The First World War
Stuart Robson   0 582 31556 5

EUROPE SINCE 1918

The Russian Revolution (Second edition)
Anthony Wood   0 582 35559 1

Lenin's Revolution: Russia, 1917–1921
David Marples   0 582 31917 X

Stalin and Stalinism (Second edition)
Martin McCauley   0 582 27658 6

The Weimar Republic (Second edition)
John Hiden   0 582 28706 5

The Inter-War Crisis 1919–1939
Richard Overy   0 582 35379 3

Fascism and the Right in Europe, 1919–1945
Martin Blinkhorn   0 582 07021 X

Spain's Civil War (Second edition)
Harry Browne   0 582 28988 2

The Third Reich (Second edition)
D G Williamson   0 582 20914 5

The Origins of the Second World War (Second edition)
R J Overy   0 582 29085 6

The Second World War in Europe
Paul MacKenzie   0 582 32692 3

Anti-Semitism before the Holocaust
Albert S Lindemann   0 582 36964 9

The Holocaust: The Third Reich and the Jews
David Engel   0 582 32720 2

Britain and Europe since 1945
Alex May   0 582 30778 3

Eastern Europe 1945–1969: From Stalinism to Stagnation
Ben Fowkes   0 582 32693 1

The Khrushchev Era, 1953–1964
Martin McCauley   0 582 27776 0

NINETEENTH-CENTURY BRITAIN

Britain before the Reform Acts: Politics and Society 1815–1832
Eric J Evans   0 582 00265 6

Parliamentary Reform in Britain c. 1770–1918
Eric J Evans   0 582 29467 3

Democracy and Reform 1815–1885
D G Wright   0 582 31400 3

Poverty and Poor Law Reform in Nineteenth-Century Britain, 1834–1914:
From Chadwick to Booth
David Englander   0 582 31554 9

The Birth of Industrial Britain: Economic Change, 1750–1850
Kenneth Morgan   0 582 29833 4

Chartism (Third edition)
Edward Royle   0 582 29080 5

Peel and the Conservative Party 1830–1850
Paul Adelman   0 582 35557 5

Gladstone, Disraeli and later Victorian Politics (Third edition)
Paul Adelman   0 582 29322 7

Britain and Ireland: From Home Rule to Independence
Jeremy Smith   0 582 30193 9

TWENTIETH-CENTURY BRITAIN

The Rise of the Labour Party 1880–1945 (Third edition)
Paul Adelman   0 582 29210 7

The Conservative Party and British Politics 1902–1951
Stuart Ball   0 582 08002 9

The Decline of the Liberal Party 1910–1931 (Second edition)
Paul Adelman   0 582 27733 7

The British Women's Suffrage Campaign 1866–1928
Harold L Smith   0 582 29811 3

War & Society in Britain 1899–1948
Rex Pope   0 582 03531 7

The British Economy since 1914: A Study in Decline?
Rex Pope   0 582 30194 7

Unemployment in Britain between the Wars
Stephen Constantine   0 582 35232 0

The Attlee Governments 1945–1951
Kevin Jefferys   0 582 06105 9

The Conservative Governments 1951–1964
Andrew Boxer   0 582 20913 7

Britain under Thatcher
Anthony Seldon and Daniel Collings   0 582 31714 2

INTERNATIONAL HISTORY

The Eastern Question 1774–1923 (Second edition)
A L Macfie   0 582 29195 X

The Origins of the First World War (Second edition)
Gordon Martel   0 582 28697 2

The United States and the First World War
Jennifer D Keene   0 582 35620 2

Anti-Semitism before the Holocaust
Albert S Lindemann   0 582 36964 9

The Origins of the Cold War, 1941–1949 (Second edition)
Martin McCauley   0 582 27659 4

Russia, America and the Cold War, 1949–1991
Martin McCauley   0 582 27936 4

The Arab–Israeli Conflict
Kirsten E Schulze   0 582 31646 4

The United Nations since 1945: Peacekeeping and the Cold War
Norrie MacQueen   0 582 35673 3

Decolonisation: The British Experience since 1945
Nicholas J White   0 582 29087 2

The Vietnam War
Mitchell Hall   0 582 32859 4

WORLD HISTORY

China in Transformation 1900–1949
Colin Mackerras   0 582 31209 4

US HISTORY

America in the Progressive Era, 1890–1914
Lewis L Gould   0 582 35671 7

The United States and the First World War
Jennifer D Keene   0 582 35620 2

The Truman Years, 1945–1953
Mark S Byrnes   0 582 32904 3

The Vietnam War
Mitchell Hall   0 582 32859 4